"*Jesus Rode a Donkey* gives us an alternative to the current culture war that divides America and its faith communities. I can't think of a better Election Day gift for my Republican—and Democratic—friends."

—**William McKinney, Ph.D.**, President, Pacific School of Religion

"You do not have to be a Republican to be a good Christian. Dr. Seger's excellent book helps make it clear that there are several strategic Biblical issues in America that are better addressed by Democrats. In the bright light of Scripture, many of us evangelicals, committed to its authority, truly dislike the forced dilemma between being a grieving Democrat or a frustrated Republican. Perhaps, as Dr. Seger reminds us, Jesus rode a donkey once, and his commands may become more clearly seen in the choices the present donkey makes for our future. Engaging some of the divine wisdom of this book could help make that happen."

—**Paul de Vries, Ph.D.**, President, New York Divinity School

"Linda Seger shows us a Christianity that overcomes divisions of liberal and conservative. But she also makes clear how liberal values are deeply rooted in the gospel message. Liberals need not think that their values are somehow less religious or Biblical than those of conservative Republicans. Seger does trenchant analyses of the conflicting values underlying conservative and liberal policy choices and asks which are closer to the values of Jesus, values rooted in love, compassion, and justice. This is an important book for this time in American life."

—**Rosemary Radford Ruether, Ph.D.**, Professor of Theology, Claremont Graduate University and Claremont School of Theology, and author of *Sexism and God-Talk* and *Integrating Ecofeminism, Globalization, and World Religions*

"A magnificent piece of work. This is one of the best evidences of scholarship, thoughtfulness, clarity, and strength. It's a winner!"

—**The Right Reverend Bennett J. Sims**, Bishop Emeritus, Episcopal Diocese of Atlanta, and author of *Servanthood: Leadership for the Third Millennium*

D0912416

"As a Baptist preacher's kid, Christian, and the only Democrat from El Paso County (an epicenter of Religious Right organizations), I am frequently compelled to point out the hypocrisy of Republican 'value based' legislation. Linda Seger's book *Jesus Rode a Donkey* has given me reams of quotes, and I have used up at least one high-lighter while reading it. It has also provided me with a strong defense against those who have at times called me 'devil worshiper,' 'sinner,' 'evil,' and—worst of all—a Democrat!"

—**Michael Merrifield**, State Representative,
District 18, El Paso County, Colorado State Legislature

"*Jesus Rode a Donkey* aptly demonstrates that no one secular political party has a lock on religious and Biblical authenticity and application. Those who are interested in this timely topic will admire Seger's effort to bring clarity and balance to American religious and political interaction."

—**William Durland, Ph.D.**,
author of *God or Nations: Radical Theology for the Religious Peace Movement*

"In this thoughtful book about crucial issues facing Americans today, Linda Seger calls for a new public discourse. Her perspective as a born-again Christian and a liberal Democrat challenges the right-wing stereotype that persons of deep faith are, or should be, conservative Republicans. *Jesus Rode a Donkey* also challenges left-wing Americans, especially liberal Christians, to affirm the vital connections between their personal faith and public policy."

—**Lloyd E. Ambrosius, Ph.D.**, Samuel Clark Waugh
Distinguished Professor of International Relations and
Professor of History, University of Nebraska

"Beyond today's polarization, Seger has written a book of lasting scholarship. The political debate about values—and whose values—may never be the same. A reference source for truth-seekers across the political spectrum."

—**Hazel Henderson**, futurist, economist, and author of
Building a Win-Win World and *Planetary Citizenship*

"In a time when cultural awareness has become a requirement for effective global engagement, and a critical element in efforts to combat the growing threat of terrorism, Linda Seger offers a thoughtful treatise on tolerance and understanding among diverse religious traditions. While her book focuses on Christianity in the modern American political context, her approach is useful to anyone seeking understanding of different religions, customs, and cultural traditions."

—**Colonel Thomas Dempsey,** U.S. Army (Retired),
a regional studies specialist with experience in conflict
resolution in both the Middle East and Africa

"In *Jesus Rode a Donkey*, Dr. Linda Seger has taken on today's 'story' of controversial partisan politics, government and religion, and the sensitive issues facing contemporary Christianity. Supported with excellent research and Biblical references, Seger provides us with a unique and fascinating critique of what it means to be a devoted follower of Christianity in America from a more liberal point of view."

—**Kate McCallum,** writer, media producer, and
founder of the Center for Conscious Creativity

"Linda Seger's book is an eloquent breath of fresh air in the political debate. *Jesus Rode a Donkey* is a clarion call for comity and peace-seeking dialogue. This book provides a well-marked path for those interested in removing the rancor and toxicity from our political discourse. In a rational world, every American President and Cabinet Secretary would be compelled to read it."

—**Robert Grant,** award-winning movie producer and writer

"This is a work of immense depth, wisdom, and subtlety. Everyone, regardless of religious or political persuasion, will be inspired by the riches offered here."

—**Jean Houston,** philosopher, social artist, teacher, and author
of *The Search for the Beloved* and *The Possible Human*

Jesus Rode
a Donkey

Jesus Rode a Donkey

Fourth Edition

Why Millions of Christians Are Democrats

Linda Seger, Th.D.

Clovercroft Publishing

Published by Clovercroft Publishing, Franklin, Tennessee. Published
in association with Larry Carpenter of Christian Book Services, LLC.
www.christianbookservices.com

This edition exactly matches the e-book published concurrently.
The 2014 second edition and the 2016 third edition
were originally published by Haven Books, LLC

Reprinted with special permission from Haven Books

Book design by Reya Patton
Text design, typesetting, and copyediting by Jean Laidig
Cover by Nick Zelinger   Author photo by Julie Gelfand

The 2006 first edition was originally published in hardcover by
Adams Media, an F+W Publications Company

ISBN: 978-1-942557-77-7 (paperback)
ISBN: 978-1-942557-81-4 (e-book)

Printed in the United States of America

Linda Seger, 4705 Hagerman Avenue, Cascade, CO 80809
719-684-0405
linda@lindaseger.com   www.LindaSeger.com

Unless otherwise noted, the Bible used as a source is the
New Jerusalem Bible, Doubleday & Company, 1973.

Dedicated to my uncle, Dr. Norman Graebner, who taught American history and American diplomacy for more than sixty years. His dedication to democracy, and his dignity and grace, have been a model to me all my life.

To my researcher, Sue Terry, who knows where to find everything—fast. I thank her for her generosity, care, and spirituality. Without her, I could not have written this book.

Contents

Acknowledgments

Thank you to my uncle, Dr. Norman Graebner, for adding quotes, giving me books, and checking facts for me. Thanks always to Sue Terry, my researcher, for her brilliance, generosity, insight, and support, and for always being there when I needed her.

A Big Thank You to my assistant, Katie Davis Gardner, for her constant dedication to making sure this book made deadlines, for discussing and clarifying concepts and words, for working long hours when necessary, for never letting me down, and always being a very helping and kind presence in my office.

Thank you to Mara Purl, my friend and great supporter of the book; Larry Carpenter and my publisher, Clovercroft; my text designer and copyeditor, Jean Laidig; my book designer, Reya Patton; and my cover designer, Nick Zelinger.

Thank you to my colleague and friend, John Winston Rainey, for his invaluable feedback and help. What a great gift! His contribution was invaluable.

Thank you to my readers for the Second Edition: Devorah Cutler-Rubenstein, Cathleen Loeser, Jonathan McPhee, Lynn Brown Rosenberg, and Pamela Jaye Smith.

For the First Edition, thank you to my fellow Christian Democrat readers, who gave me copious notes and wonderful insights: Pamela Jaye Smith, Kim Peterson, Cathleen

Loeser, Bobbie Sue Nave, and Jim Nave. For the First Edition, thank you to my Christian Republican reader, Debra Weitala, who tells me she is now a registered Democrat! And thanks to my Republican neighbor Steve Berendt for our ten-hour day filled with stimulating discussions of ideas and with his brilliant suggestions for honing the language of the book.

For the First Edition, thank you to Dr. Cheri Junk for help with Chapters 1 and 2, to Kristin Howard for her help with Chapter 1, to Tirtza and Abe Weschler for help on Chapter 3, to Ann Grant Martin and Pam Jones for their comments on Chapter 6, and to Devorah Cutler-Rubenstein for help with Chapters 7 and 8.

For the First Edition, thanks to my agent, Janet Benrey, and to Sarah Callbeck, Martha Callbeck, and Laurie Wagner Byers.

To my Quaker friend, Dr. Bill Durland, Ph.D. in politics and religion, who has guided me through several chapters; to my neighbor Tom Radcliffe, who has worked in the White House under several administrations and helped with the chapter titled "Secrets, Lies, and Deceptions"; and to William Flavin from the U.S. Army War College, who provided me with many papers and fact checks in the "War and Peace" chapter—thanks.

And thanks always to my husband, Peter Hazen Le Var, for reading chapters and for continuing to love me despite knowing what life is like when I'm writing a book!

Note: In order to be inclusive, most of my biblical quotes come from the New Jerusalem Bible, which is used by Catholics and Protestants alike. Very occasionally, another translation is used.

Introduction

By the time we are born, we have already been impacted by the political decisions that our parents and their parents and the founding fathers have made. These choices determine the opportunities we have, the visions and dreams we follow, the philosophies we will accept, and our understanding of what needs to be changed. It doesn't take long for us to become little political beings with opinions about how we're supposed to vote and what party we're supposed to belong to.

I grew up as a Republican. I remember being a grade school student in the 1950s when everybody liked Ike. It was presumed that everybody would vote for Eisenhower because of what he had done for our country in the past, and because he was a nice, likable man. When we had our grade school mock elections, there were only two people in my grade school class who voted for Adlai Stevenson. After staring at them for a few moments, I reached some conclusions that these two people were not like us. Many years later I discovered that my uncle, who was an author and a renowned university professor in history, felt Stevenson was one of our truly great Americans. He had been an avid supporter of Stevenson, and was a Democrat. But I knew nothing of that at an early age.

By the time I could think further about politics, Nixon

and John F. Kennedy were running against each other. It seemed to me absolutely essential for Nixon to win. I was told that if Kennedy won, the Pope would move into the White House and govern our country, because a Roman Catholic had to obey the Pope above our Constitution, above our Congress, and above any other democratic institution that might not be quite in line with the Pope's point of view.

But Kennedy won me over. His vision of putting a man on the moon, his creation of the Peace Corps, and his strength and charisma made me excited about political leadership. In my developing adolescence, I almost became a Democrat in my mind, even though I was not able to vote. Lyndon B. Johnson turned me back to the Republicans because of his coarse and sometimes bullying personality. It was many years later that I realized how much good he had done for our country. I moved back and forth and finally, with the corruption of the Nixon Watergate scandal, I registered first as an Independent and then as a Democrat.

When I went to seminary in the 1970s, I came into contact with some new ways of thinking that developed my consciousness. By that time, my mother had already moved over to the Democratic Party because of the influence of a minister, and because of her developing anti-war feelings. My sister and my father remained staunch Republicans.

When I was in seminary, even though I worked three jobs, studied all the rest of the time, and had some scholarship help, I was so poor I couldn't afford to park at a parking meter because I didn't have an extra dime. I went on the food stamps program, and food stamps saved me. They made it possible for me to stay in graduate school and to eventually get my Th.D. Experiencing what it was like to be poor changed how I thought about government assistance. No matter how hard I worked, I still needed help. I believed it was to the benefit of me and my country for me to complete graduate school. At one point, one of my jobs gave me a raise of $20.00, which disqualified me for food stamps. Within two weeks, my employer illegally fired me. It took me six weeks to get back on the food stamp program. The day before the food stamps arrived, I looked through my cupboard. All I had left was dry cereal, which I ate that day with water.

During this time, I was also grateful for free women's clinics, which gave me the opportunity to see a doctor when ill and to receive medications, if necessary. Now that I'm over 65, I am grateful for Medicare and for the Social Security check I have just started to collect.

My developing view of the government's role in helping its citizens was reaffirmed in 2004 when my sister became ill with ALS (Lou Gehrig's Disease). She was eligible for Medicaid because ALS is one of those few diseases where one can get Medicaid before 65, but the social service agencies were not responding quickly. I was told to call Holly's representative from Long Island, New York, who was Steve Israel, a Democrat. His response changed my sister's life. He and his office staff helped her get a Medicaid card within a week. They were compassionate, efficient, caring, and on top of the problem. Although she died several years later, the political policy that allowed her to get the help she needed made it possible for her to die with grace and dignity. This assistance from Steve Israel made such a powerful impact that her daughter, who had never voted for anyone except a Republican, voted for him, and said, "I voted for him because he helped my mom."

Many times we make changes in the way we think about political policy because of personal influences including the people we meet, the jobs we have, the books we read, and those who help us form our theology and our understanding of the Bible.

I work in the film industry, and I live in the context of an industry that is made up of agnostics and atheists and Jews and Christians and Muslims and Buddhists and New Agers. I cannot live and work in this world if I'm intolerant of different points of view, because my work demands teamwork with a diverse group of people from all over the world.

The big issues of the day, such as racism, sexism, classism, ecology, and war, began to push me toward registering as a Democrat. I found Democrats, as a whole, more compassionate and tolerant. I learned that those who needed help were far beyond a stereotype of "takers" and "dependants." The help was usually not a hand out but a hand up. At the same time, I became clearer about my own identity as a Christian, affirming the guidance of the Holy Spirit, the involvement in our world of Jesus Christ, and the necessity for me to develop a more social and global consciousness.

It is said that the conservative mind and the liberal mind are quite different. Perhaps they are. Some say that the staunch Republican and the staunch Democrat are almost like two different species because they have different values and visions of the future, and different ways of interpreting the Bible and message of Jesus. For many years, this difference has evolved into an opinion that a Christian could not possibly be anything except a Republican. Republican policies and Republican speeches that mention religion imply (and sometimes state absolutely) that the Republican Party carries the message of Jesus, and that the poor Democrats have lost the point and have obviously gone very far astray.[1]

We form our spiritual opinions about politics in different ways. Most Christians look at what Scripture says about issues. What does the Scripture say about the poor? Abortion? The environment? Helping the mentally and physically ill? Homosexuality? Education? Social programs for the poor and disadvantaged?

To what extent might Biblical translations, the meanings of words, and the context of the time change our viewpoint?

Some Christians, particularly Catholics, look to Church tradition and practice. How did the church fathers and mothers, saints, and historical practices address various issues? Did those interpretations change or remain the same through the ages? What are the influences that change our minds? How are new understandings guided by the Holy Spirit?

This book is written as a kind of Christian Political Apologetic. It is meant to clarify what we, as Christian Democrats, believe and why we believe it. Originally, it was an assignment from Adams Media Publishers, who wanted a book which would respond to the oft-repeated idea that the Christian vote was the Republican vote. Since I was a Christian Democrat with a theology background and experience as an author, they asked if I'd be willing to write a book articulating how we use our Christian values to inform our political decisions.

In this Third Edition, I have updated some of the political information, although the focus of Democrats and

Republicans has been fairly consistent since I started researching this topic in 2005. However, this year shows some of the sharpest divisions of the values and actions between Republicans and Democrats.

I felt it was essential to do a 2016 Edition because it is an important and groundbreaking election. Hillary Clinton may be the first woman president, and she may be one of the best-qualified candidates who have ever run for office. She brings her experience and knowledge base as a lawyer for the poor and disenfranchised, a governor's wife who knows the workings of a state, a president's wife who discussed issues and advised her husband, and as someone who researched and created health care policy, a senator, a secretary of state, and a presidential candidate twice. She knows the world—the international leaders and the way Congress works. She has proven she knows how to cross party lines and how to be strong and firm. She has influence and understands the potential of diplomacy. She is the only candidate who would be ready on Day One.

Bernie Sanders has long worked for a more equal economic system, for equality in our justice system, for a raise in the minimum wage, and for peace policies. He was one of the few who voted against George W. Bush's Iraq War, which was considered by many to be one of the wiser votes in Congress.

Their views and policies are clear.

In the 2014 Edition, I changed the subtitle. Originally, the subtitle was *Why the Republicans Don't Have the Corner on Christ,* which was the publisher's choice. Although I didn't like the divisiveness implied in this subtitle, I recognized it was a direct response to the prevailing presumptions of

2006. In the last two editions, with the new subtitle, I have tried to remove some of the divisiveness of the first edition.

This book is written for Democrats who identify as Christians, to help them better understand how their spirituality leads them to political choices. I expect that some people who are spiritual but not necessarily Christian might also find this book helpful. The previous editions were read by many Independents and some Republicans who said they liked the book, and I hope some Independents and Republicans will read this edition as well. Perhaps, for them, it will open up a better understanding of why their brothers and sisters in Christ vote differently than they do. Perhaps it might break down some of the barriers and divisiveness that exist between parties and people. It may lead to all of us working together for a more loving nation. And for some, it may change their vote.

If you are unsure about which party and which policies best express your values, perhaps this book will bring you to some new decisions about who you are, what you believe as a citizen of our country and of our world, and what actions you can take to help create a society that is an expression of God's grace, the love of Christ, and the manifestation of the Holy Spirit.

Chapter One

How Would Jesus Vote?

"[You] have neglected the weightier matters
of the Law—justice, mercy, good faith!"
Matthew 23:23

Jesus and the prophets shared a vision for a people and a nation—that a nation would respond to its people with justice and mercy and good faith. These Christian values are also democratic values, asking us to come together to create a free, equal, and kind society that cares for all its citizens. We are asked to help remove structures that oppress its citizens. Christian values recognize the redemptive potential and possibilities of humanity. So does democracy. A democratic nation provides a voice for the majority as well as the minority, and promises freedom and protection for all. A democratic nation, founded on religious principles, struggles to create unity out of diversity, without compromising either one.

Which Is the Christian Political Party?

Both the Republican and Democratic parties, and some of the others as well, are made up of millions of Christians. But categorizing Christians is not so easy, since Christians fall into a number of different groups.

Fundamentalist Christians believe that every word in the Bible is the literal Word of God. Evangelical Christians believe that we must be Born Again by accepting Jesus Christ as our personal Savior, and that their work on earth is to spread the Gospel of Christ to all nations. Mainstream Protestants and Catholics, and many liberal and progressive Christians, believe that the true Word of God is not the Bible but Christ Jesus, who continues to reveal Himself and transform us. They see the Bible as inspired, but they are not literalists. They believe God's work continues to develop and unfold in our modern world.

Christian Mystics put the focus on the Holy Spirit dwelling within. Some Mystics have visions and ecstatic experiences of the Living Christ. Some of these, such as the Quakers (including me), combine their Mystical devotions with social actions, believing that the work of the Spirit within leads us naturally to manifesting the work of the Spirit in the world.

Some Christians put their focus on the life and sayings of Jesus, and see him as a good man who is our model for a good life, but don't see him as the Son of God. Nevertheless, they identify as Christian.

Some of these Christians, such as Catholics and mainstream Protestants and liberal Christians, are more apt to vote Democrat. Others, such as Fundamentalists and Evangelicals, are more apt to vote Republican. But the actual voting statistics are not quite so neat.

About one out of five Christian Evangelicals votes Democrat. The foremost evangelist of our time—Billy Graham—is a Democrat. In 2004, Catholics, and other Protestants, on the whole, were almost equally divided between George W. Bush, who is a Methodist, and John Kerry, who is a Catholic. In 2008 and 2012, black Protestants voted overwhelmingly for Barack Obama. Obama also got the Jewish vote and 75% of the Hispanic Catholic vote, with Catholics on the whole being almost evenly divided between Republicans and Democrats, and Protestants tending slightly toward the Republican Party. Clearly, in all elections, millions of Christians in both parties vote their values and their priorities.[1]

How Do We Judge our Candidates?

Christians have many ideas on how to decide the best way to express their Christian values and faith through the way they vote. Many begin by figuring out whether the candidate is a Christian like them. All the candidates in 2016 are Christian except for Bernie Sanders, who is Jewish. They come from a wide variety of denominations. Hillary Clinton is Methodist. Jeb Bush was Methodist until he converted to Catholicism. Ben Carson is Seventh Day Adventist, Donald Trump is Presbyterian, and Ted Cruz is Southern Baptist. Marco Rubio was a Mormon for a few years in his youth and now attends both a Roman Catholic church and a Southern Baptist church. John Kasich is Anglican.

Some voters look at the candidates and judge whether they express the gifts of the Holy Spirit, such as love, peace, joy, gentleness, self-control, trustfulness, faithfulness, patience, and goodness.[2]

Voters might ask: What is the Good these candidates have done in the world? Have they helped feed the hungry, clothed the naked, given a cup of cold water to the thirsty, and given hope to the hopeless?[3] Have they cared about the 'least of these' as Jesus asked them to? What and whom do they care about? Have they made the world a better place? Have they built up God's Kingdom—not just with words, but with deeds? Whom do they serve? God—or power, money, and the elite?

Christians also judge candidates to see if they are expressing qualities that are contrary to the Spirit. These include the Seven Deadly Sins of pride, envy, greed, gluttony, lust, anger, and sloth as well as bragging, mean-spiritedness, fear, dishonesty, and hate.[4]

Why are these sins so dangerous? Because they hook the basest part of our human nature and drag us into the pit of nastiness. We are then tempted to participate and hit back since we've been hit. We want to give tit for tat. The ugly mess spreads.

We only have to look at the Republican debates in the 2016 election season to see what happens when one person begins with nastiness and malice. Donald Trump set the tone for the Republicans. He attacked, Labeled. Called others names. And kept the focus on the fight, not the issues. For a while, other candidates tried to stay out of the fray—and Kasich and Carson managed to keep their cool. But others got hooked. Trump's followers found it thrilling. Finally there was someone who spoke to their anger and fear. The more he stoked the fires, the more excited they became. He was their guy. Their savior. He was going to make America great again, in one vague way or another, and he was going to hit every bully they wanted hit, and be the Power that would stand up for them. He spoke with force, and attacked and diverted every attack against him. Jesus was right—"What goes into a man's mouth does not make him unclean, but what comes out of his mouth, that is what makes him unclean."[5] And there is a lot of vitriol coming out of a lot of mouths this season. But it isn't just the person attacking who is unclean, it's the people in his way who are victims of this unhealthiness. They can easily become corrupted, either by weakening because the attack demoralizes them and strips them of their power (this happened to Jeb Bush—Trump knew just how to get his goat) or because they decide to play the same nasty game, which is happening to Cruz and Rubio. Their worst instincts have been hooked—and they exchange one blood threat and attack for another, not yet realizing that no one can out-Trump Trump. He is a master at this. And the game is like a great bullfight, or cock fight, or gladiator fight. Blood is drawn. People who are lured into the slough lose their identity as children of God. If we want to see Christian behavior, we won't see it in these exchanges.

As this nastiness spreads out, voters get caught up in the bloody game, and at some point, the international community gets caught up too—slash for slash, burn for burn. And our world, which already teeters on the edge of disharmony and hatred, tilts toward destruction.

That is exactly what Jesus, and Paul, and the prophets

warned us about. Sin is crouching at our door, it desires to have us, but we must master it.[6]

As my Texan friend sometimes says to me, "Don't get none of this on ya."

I personally am amazed by the Evangelical support for Donald Trump, who has been called "Hater in Chief" by *Esquire* Magazine and whose bragging and pride are so overt. Trump knows little about the Bible; he has stumbled when asked what is his favorite verse of the Bible. He's said he never asks for forgiveness because he's not making mistakes. And when he speaks about the Lord's Supper, he says he likes his little wafer and wine at communion because it makes him feel good.[7] On Bill O'Reilly's show in January 2016, Trump expressed his Christian value system as being about an-eye-for-an-eye. O'Reilly turned his cheek and said that was from the Old Testament, and that the New Kingdom of Christ brought in the idea of turning the other cheek. Donald Trump shrugged as if he had no idea of what O'Reilly was talking about.

A number of Evangelical Christians are beginning to speak against Donald Trump and to show their concerns from a Christian perspective. Russell Moore, the President of the Ethics and Religious Liberty Commission of the Southern Baptist Convention, says, "Trump's vitriolic—and often racist and sexist—language about immigrants. women, the disabled and others ought to concern anyone who believes that all persons . . . are created in God's image." Moore discussed Trump's "narcissistic pursuit of power," calling it "decadent" and "deviant." And he said for voters "to view it any other way now would be for them to lose their soul."[8]

A number of noted Evangelicals have said, publicly, they won't support Trump if he is nominated. This leaves Conservative Evangelical Christians in an ethical dilemma, since everything points to Trump as the Republican nominee. They could join the 20% of other Evangelical Christians and vote Democrat, at least for the Presidential candidate. Even Republicans would have to admit that Democrats have conducted their campaign with more civility and concern for the poor, the needy, widows and orphans, and the "least of these" than Trump. They might decide not to vote, thereby not adding their voice to the democratic process. They might decide to vote for other candidates on the ballot and leave the Presidential candidate blank or add a write-in candidate. They might decide to vote for him, but if he truly is dangerous, immoral, and a hateful force in American politics, they would be colluding with evil. Perhaps as more Christian voices express their concern during the primaries, there will be a profound turn in the direction of the 2016 campaign. But I have my doubts.

The Struggle for Unity

If we move beyond party to people, a Christian Democrat and a Christian Republican might agree on many issues. Sometimes they vote according to whom they feel they can best trust to keep promises. They vote for the person who seems to have the same priorities as they do, or the one they think can best exemplify these values in our government. Many vote for the issues, while trying to assess the character of the candidate.

Both democracy and Christianity are challenging. They challenge us to go against our seemingly natural human behaviors of hatred, intolerance, greed, and self-righteousness, or what the Apostle Paul lists as the problems when the Holy Spirit is not at work: "antagonisms, rivalry, . . . bad temper and quarrels, disagreements, factions and malice"[9]—all the traits we see daily on our television sets, read about almost daily in our newspapers, and often see manifested in election campaigns.

On the surface, there seem to be issues that are not easily resolved, because there seems to be an inner contradiction between Christianity and democracy. Churches often ask us to be homogeneous in our beliefs and actions. Churches have creeds, and dogmas, and statements of belief, and the members are asked to, at least verbally, agree with them. But our country is not homogeneous. From the beginning, settlers of our country came to America to find freedom, and soon found that there was a diverse group of others, all of whom wanted the same freedom for themselves. Early on, many of the settlers respected these differences in order to create a democratic system.

We are often in a struggle between the desire to be inclusive and the desire to be exclusive. We often feel a struggle between our natural suspicion of each other and the command to love our neighbor.

I have heard time and again that we are a Christian nation. But we are not a Christian nation—neither in many of our actions nor in the makeup of our citizens. No matter how much we might like to be homogeneous in religion, we are not. We are a diverse nation, made up of Christians, Jews, Buddhists, Muslims, Hindus, Wiccans, Hare

Krishnas, Sikhs, New Agers, atheists, agnostics, Zoroaster followers, and followers of Native American spirituality, among others.

There are many people other than Christians who have values. Many of those values are similar to ours—among them, the values of freedom, equality, honesty, justice, mercy, compassion, and the Golden Rule. Many people besides Christians see America as the land of opportunity, the land where they can achieve their dreams. Although there may be more of "us" than "them," and although our democracy may have been founded mainly (but not entirely) by Christians, our country has strived from the very beginning to give freedom and justice to all. As Christians living in a democratic nation, what we desire for ourselves must be available for all. Suppressing another's freedom is not the answer.

Was Jesus Political?

Christians look to God to lead and guide them in their decisions. They look to the example of Jesus, but some wonder if Jesus is relevant to our political choices.

On the surface, it might seem as if Jesus was not a political person but was someone who focused, instead, on individuals and individual relationships. He certainly did not live up to the Jewish hopes for a political Messiah. The Jews in Jesus' day imagined a militant Messiah who would lead an army, overthrow the oppressive rule of Rome, and establish a religious kingdom.

We can, however, see some of the political viewpoints of

Jesus through the actions he took and those he didn't take. Jesus didn't identify with any of the political structures of the day. He rejected the Sadducees, the conservatives who were willing to go along with foreign domination provided it didn't compromise their position. He confronted the Pharisees, who observed religious practices in great detail, made hundreds of oppressive religious laws, and also supported the established powers of the day. He never joined the Essenes, who rejected political involvement and took no part in any of the religious ceremonies they considered impure. Essenes formed a separate sect, and moved to Qumran by the Dead Sea. He was not part of the Zealots, one of the most politically active groups. They were nationalists, who wanted a radical transformation of existing political institutions through violent revolution.

Many of Jesus' followers were from different political parties with different political and religious beliefs. Simon, called the Zealot, would have either been a revolutionary or a sympathizer with the group that desired to overthrow the Roman government. Matthew, the tax collector, worked for the oppressive government Simon wanted to overthrow. Yet there's no evidence that Jesus tried to change their political parties, or even their religion. He wanted to change their hearts and their actions.[10]

Was Jesus Conservative or Liberal?

The labels of conservative and liberal can paint individuals into a corner. Liberals often hold conservative values, and those considered to be conservative often hold certain liberal values.

The word "conservative" comes from the word "conserve," which means to preserve. Generally, conservatives want to preserve the status quo. They prefer to maintain existing habits and views and institutions. A true conservative usually wants government to have a limited role in social and economic affairs. At their best, conservatives ground our country by recognizing the ideals of the past and giving us a solid foundation on which to stand.

At their worst, conservatives can be inflexible, rigid, legalistic, and immovable, with no vision of a future and little thought to how our actions today might affect the world of tomorrow. They are sometimes fearful of risks and distrustful of change. Because they are often unable to imagine other possibilities or to believe that change can lead us to a better society, conservatives are less apt to envision new ways to solve social problems.

"Liberal" is a word coming from the Latin *liberare*—to set free or to liberate. The word often means generous and bounteous and open-handed, as used when someone gives liberally to charity. Liberals tend to advocate reforms that would achieve greater freedom for citizens. To achieve that, they are more apt to criticize the status quo, imagine new possibilities, and ask how it can be done better. They are willing to be unconventional and untraditional in order to solve a problem. At their most extreme, liberals can become so freedom-minded that their actions lead to excess, anarchy, and a lack of restraint that can become destructive.

We sometimes hear the term "progressive," and sometimes politicians such as Hillary Clinton refer to themselves as progressives rather than liberals. They tend to be tolerant of others and want to remove restraints to the freedom of all citizens, not just for themselves. They want to improve the world and improve the social welfare of others. "Progressive Christianity," a relatively new term, refers to Christians who work toward a more just and compassionate world and struggle against racism, sexism, homophobia, and other human oppressions. They recognize that there is truth in other traditions as well, and they strive to overcome dogmatism.

All of these positions need to be balanced. Lacking balance, any position can lead to the vicious extremism we see in almost all political parties and religions—ranging from the fundamentalists who will kill in the name of their party or their religion, to the radicals who destroy property and create anarchy in the name of freedom.

Like most of us, Jesus exemplified both conservative and liberal values. There were certain values he wanted to conserve; there were others that he wanted to liberate from a rule-oriented culture in order to reinterpret, broaden, or change them.

The Freedom to Love God

The most important value that Jesus wanted to conserve was the commandment to "Love the Lord your God with all your heart, with all your soul, with all your mind, and all your strength."[11] Love of God is above all things and is the guiding principle throughout the entire Bible. How to love

God has been one of the thorniest issues any individual confronts.

Our nation was founded by many who loved God. Before the Constitution was written, the early colonies tried to legislate the love of God. They became repressive when they tried to impose laws about how this love was to be shown. The Massachusetts Bay Colony persecuted any who didn't love God in the same way they did. They banished those who didn't agree with them, particularly the Quakers. Besides being banished, Quakers were imprisoned, whipped, branded, burned, and enslaved; some had their ears cut off and their property confiscated; several were put to death for insisting on the right to worship in their own way.[12]

Puritan minister Roger Williams (who later helped found the first Baptist church in America) was banished from Boston because he believed that everyone had the right to think and worship as he pleased. In his pamphlet called "The Bloudy Tenent of Persecution, for the Cause of Conscience," published in 1644, Williams said, "How ghastly and unbelieved . . . was the damage done and the number of innocent human beings slaughtered in the effort to make men and women worship God in some certain way."[13]

He believed in separation of church and state so neither could control the other, and complete toleration by the government of all sorts of religion, even the religion of the Native Americans. Williams, the Quakers, and other tolerant Christians established freedom of worship and freedom from a state-sponsored religion.

Just as important as Williams' ideals about religious freedom were his ideals about democracy. He believed that governing was not the work of the aristocracy, but that each family should have an equal voice in the government. Together with Anne Hutchinson and Samuel Gorton, he founded Rhode Island, which was one of the first colonies with complete religious freedom.

In 1657, the Flushing Remonstrance was created as a declaration of religious freedom in New York, and an affirmation of diversity. It is considered to be one of the precursors of the Bill of Rights, and declares, "we are bound by the Law to do good unto all men," and guarantees that "love, peace and liberty" should be extended to all residents, including "to Jews, Turks and Egyptians as they are considered the sons of Adam . . . our desire is not to offend one of his little ones in whatsoever form, name or title he appears in, whether Presbyterian, Independent, Baptist or Quaker, but shall be glad to see anything of God in any of them, desiring to do unto all men as we desire all men should do unto us, which is the true law both of Church and State."

In the constitutional debates almost a century and a half later, the issue of religious freedom was still in the forefront. Those who preferred the Articles of Confederation to the Constitution felt the Constitution didn't take religion seriously enough. They believed that society should be a "molder of character, rather than . . . a regulator of conduct." Those who favored the Articles of Confederation believed that one religion should mold everyone into their same value system, and make laws to ensure that everyone behaved in a proper religious manner.

The writers of the Constitution didn't want to legislate religion. They said, "little democracies can no more be ruled by prayer than large ones." They recognized that

"Men act mainly from passion and interest. . . . The Constitution was deliberately and properly designed not to try to stifle or transform those motives . . . but to channel them in the direction of the public good."[14] The Founders saw that diversity was a protection against the coercion that can happen from majority rule.

Thomas Jefferson said, "Difference of opinion is advantageous in religion. The several sects perform the office of a censor . . . over such other. Is uniformity attainable? Millions of innocent men, women and children, since the introduction of Christianity have been burnt, tortured, fined, imprisoned; yet we have not advanced one inch toward uniformity. What has been the effect of coercion? To make one half of the world fools and the other half hypocrites."[15]

Jefferson was concerned about the government getting too involved in individual opinions and belief systems. He said, ". . . religion is a matter which lies solely between man and his God, that he owes account to none other for his faith or his worship, that the legitimate powers of government reach actions only, and not opinions. I contemplate . . . their legislature should make no law respecting an establishment of religion, or prohibiting the free exercise thereof."[16]

The writers of the Constitution didn't want to legislate religion. They recognized that democracies cannot be ruled by prayer.

Abraham Lincoln said, "Most governments have been based, practically, on the denial of equal rights of men . . . ours began, by affirming those rights."[17] There was a constant tension between developing a country toward a theocracy, with a state religion, or toward a democracy, where diversity was accepted. Throughout our history, the impulse toward religious diversity could not be stifled. If anything, persecution strengthened the dissent and fostered the drive toward the separation of church and state.

Religious tolerance and diversity won, hoping to promote an open and accepting society.

Challenges to Religious Freedom

One of the clearest definitions between the Republican and Democratic values lies with the question of what part religion should play in a nation. The Democrats have had a fairly consistent policy to protect our religious freedoms. Republicans have, during some previous administrations, been protective of religious freedom. However, within the Republican Party is a group who wants to remove our freedom of religion. They are called the Dominionists, and they believe they are called to bring the government under the dominion of one particular brand of Christianity.

The movement was begun by D. James Kennedy in Florida in 1959. (Kennedy also helped found the Moral Majority in 1979 along with the Rev. Jerry Falwell and others.) Sarah Palin is a Dominionist. Others who are Dominionists or have Dominionist leanings are Sam Brownback, Ralph Reed, Michelle Bachmann, Ted Cruz, and Rand Paul.

Kennedy said, "Our job is to reclaim America for Christ, whatever the cost. As the vice regents of God, we are to exercise godly dominion and influence over our neighborhoods, our schools, our government, our literature and arts, our sports arenas, our entertainment media, our news media, our scientific endeavors—in short, over every aspect and institution of human society."[18]

There is nothing wrong with bringing values into every aspect of our social and political life. That's what we would want in a country that tries to serve the Good. But Kennedy was not talking about trying to make Christianity more prevalent in American political policy; rather, he promoted the sole use of the Dominionist brand of Christianity in making public policy—to the exclusion of not only other faiths, but also other interpretations of Christianity. This kind of exclusion and lack of protection for those unlike themselves is unconstitutional and unjust. I can imagine a prayer from a teacher or preacher that says, "Our Lord and Commander, we ask that you give your power to the troops in Iraq and Afghanistan and Syria, and help them to overcome the enemy as we fight this great Crusade to lead us to truth."

I have heard prayers like this. To me, it's a self-righteous prayer that makes nationalism a religion, rather than Christianity. It sees The Other as the enemy, rather than as The Neighbor, and it implies there will be hundreds, if not hundreds of thousands, of the enemy killed in the name of Jesus. It gives no room for my own Christian belief system as a pacifist.

I can imagine another kind of prayer, that would be anathema to most conservatives, and perhaps millions of other Christians as well: "Our Ground of all being, Mother Earth, Father Sky, embrace our bodies and bring us into unity with you." Although this may be a more loving prayer, it is so vague and unspecific that it would be meaningless to many. Yet, I have also heard prayers such as this.

I can imagine nationalist prayers that would insist on our complete loyalty to our president, even when he is lying and covering up treasonous or illegal or immoral activities. Do we really want to be saying state-sponsored prayers that keep us from questioning Watergate? Or the Iran–Contra illegal deals? Or the prison abuse in Iraq, Afghanistan, and Guantánamo Bay?

What about classrooms where most of the students are not Christian but Jewish, or Buddhist or Muslim, or not religious at all? Does the majority rule? Will we all be asked to chant or will the non-Christians be forced to pray "in Jesus' name"?

Luis Palau, an evangelical preacher who is close to Billy Graham, bristles at the coarseness of these calls for absolute power. Palau is concerned about the ways this influential Republican Christian group belittles homosexuals, "effete" intellectuals and secular humanists. Palau says, "If we become called to Christ, we will build an effective nation through personal ethics. When you lead a life of purity, when you respect your wife and are good to your family, when you don't waste money gambling and womanizing, you begin to work for better schools, for more protection and safety from your community. All change, historically, comes from the bottom up."[19]

Other evangelical Christians are equally concerned about this movement. Former Senator Mark Pryor, an evangelical Christian, says, "It is presumptuous of them [the Christian Right] to think they represent all Christians in America, even to say they represent all evangelical Christians."[20]

C. S. Lewis, the Protestant writer and theologian, said he believed in democracy "because I believe in the Fall of Man.

I think most people [want democracy] for the opposite reason. A great deal of democratic enthusiasm descends from the ideas of people . . . who believed in democracy because they thought mankind so wise and good that everyone deserved a share in the government. The danger of defending democracy on those grounds is that they're not true. . . . I find that they're not true without looking further than myself. I don't deserve a share in governing a hen-roost, much less a nation. Nor do most people. . . . The real reason for democracy is . . . Mankind is so fallen that no man can be trusted with unchecked power over his fellows. Aristotle said that some people were only fit to be slaves. I do not contradict him. But I reject slavery because I see no men fit to be masters."[21]

Upholding True Conservative Values

Jesus was both conservative and liberal. A conservative value that Jesus affirmed was the value of accountability and responsibility. Leaders are to rule justly, not be beholden to the rich, the powerful, or the influential. Justice transcends political parties.

Both political parties have had a number of presidents, and members of Congress, who have lied, deceived, and tried to get away with breaking laws. It is a right and righteous act to hold these people accountable. In these circumstances, unfortunately, instead of truth-telling, blaming became the focus of the discussions.

The Bible also begins with a commandment that none of the prophets, nor Jesus nor Paul, have overturned—the commandment to tend the environment that God has given us. Although this is a conservative value, it has been adopted by those considered liberals. We are asked to conserve, preserve, and care for the world. Noah went to considerable trouble, under God's command, to make sure that the animals didn't become extinct. Jesus extols the beauty of the lilies of the field and the birds of the air, telling us that God will care for us, as He cares for nature. If there is one Christian value that should transcend political parties, it should be our care for the environment.

There is a great deal said about money in the Bible—much of it about giving money to the poor and about letting our money work for us.[22] Our country rarely follows these values—spending more than it has, not caring enough for the needy, only rarely creating surpluses.

We love money. It defines us as powerful and comfortable and important. We use it to gain political favor and to increase our clout. We spend it easily. We deny it to some, give a great deal of it to others. We hide and waste a great deal of it. Elections are often funded by the very rich exerting considerable control over the outcome, far out of proportion to their numbers.

Have we been good stewards of our money? The Republican Party used to be considered the party of fiscal responsibility, but this has not been true since the beginning of Ronald Reagan's presidency. President Reagan ran up the national debt to historic proportions, followed by Presidents George H. W. Bush and George W. Bush.

Fiscal responsibility is usually considered a conservative value, although the Democratic Party has been more fiscally responsible than the Republican Party for more than thirty-five years. From 1981, when Reagan's first budget took effect, until 1993, when Bill Clinton became president, the Republicans ballooned the debt. Part of the debt under Clinton was 2.2 trillion dollars of interest because of the Reagan–Bush debt. Clinton left a surplus of about 523 billion dollars by the end of his term. Economists projected that at the rate we were going, we could pay off the entire national debt by 2012. But George W. Bush stopped this process and again ran up the debt.

When George Bush took office, the House was Democratic and the Senate was split 50–50. The Congress suggested a budget that was 20 billion dollars less than what Bush requested. George Bush then ran up the debt because of the two wars that he began and his tax cuts which mainly benefited the rich. George W. Bush took control of the budget on October 1, 2001 when the debt was 5.8 trillion dollars, and his last budget year ended October 1, 2009, leaving the next president, Barack Obama, with a debt of 11.9 trillion dollars. Since Obama's first budget in 2009, the debt has continued to grow, partly because of the recession which began under Bush, partly because of the interest on the debt, and entitlements such as Social Security and Medicare. If Bush had not taken us into two expensive wars, we would have had a surplus and we would have been able to pay for the social programs that have suffered many cuts in the last few years.[23]

It is estimated that the policies of the 2016 Republican candidates would balloon the debt, favor the wealthy, and further cut social programs. All of the major candidates believe their policies would stimulate the economy by giving money to the wealthy, which would create jobs, and the money would trickle down to the middle class. This is called "trickle down economics," and during the last 35 years it's been proven wrong.

Pope Francis has denounced this "trickle down" economic theory on moral grounds and sees it as part of an overall policy that puts money above people. Certainly, it favors the rich and diminishes the importance of the poor.

According to the Citizens for Tax Justice and the Tax Foundation, Donald Trump would swell the National Debt by 10-12 trillion and the "richest 1% would receive a 27% increase in their incomes." Trump's idea to complete the wall between Mexico and the United States is estimated to cost over 12 billion and perhaps as much as 15–25 billion dollars. It would then take another 750 million a year to maintain the wall and another 1.4 billion dollars to add the necessary border patrol personnel. Trump intends to have Mexico pay twelve billion dollars to build the wall, something they couldn't afford. He would threaten to change our trade agreements if they didn't, which would leave Mexico even poorer and Mexicans more desperate and more eager to emigrate. This is not feasible for improved international relations nor for helping the poor and dispossessed.[24]

Both Hillary Clinton and Bernie Sanders want to increase the taxes for the wealthy, who are often defined as those in the top one-tenth of 1% or 1% of the population, or sometimes defined as those making more than $250,000 a year.

The plans of Marco Rubio and Ted Cruz would add between 768 billion and 12 trillion dollars to the National Debt over the next decade, and both these plans would favor the most wealthy.[25]

The Liberal Values of Jesus

Although both the Republican and Democratic parties contain conservatives and liberals, the Republican Party has increasingly sided with its more conservative members.

Our country was founded on liberal and liberating values. The Founding Fathers were willing to change the status quo, overthrow an oppressive government, and create a new form of government by the people, of the people, for the people.

All men are created equal under God, but in the period of time leading up to 1860, they were born into an unequal system. Only white men who owned property enjoyed inalienable rights. Blacks were considered three-fifths of a person. Married women had almost no civil rights at all. Many Christians, but not all, supported this idea, quoting the Bible to justify slavery and oppression of women. Many Christians limited and resisted extending equal rights to others.

How did this change? Through the work of more liberal Christians. Most of the first abolitionists were Christians—mainly Quakers, Methodists, and Congregationalists. Over time, the impulse to liberate women also grew from Christian roots.

The most recent and extraordinary example of this process was the civil rights movement in the twentieth century, led by a Baptist minister, Dr. Martin Luther King Jr. The movement was conceived in African-American churches and sustained by Christians of all racial and ethnic groups. Many Christians have been, and continue to be, at the forefront of the fight for the civil rights for others.

Throughout the Gospels, we see the portrait of Jesus as a man who questioned the prevailing religious and social establishment. Many actions that Jesus took, and stories that he told, were about liberating people from legal, religious, and governmental oppression. Rather than demanding adherence to religious dogmas and the hundreds of religious laws, he questioned the way things were, and followed the freer Law of Love.

Jesus transcended sexism when he talked to a woman at the well in Samaria.[26] Men were not supposed to interact with women except within the family, yet he spoke theology to a woman of a despised class and understood her. He affirmed Mary's desire to listen and to learn, rather than fill the traditional woman's role played by her sister, Martha.[27] Women followed him around the countryside and he accepted them, even though this would have been against the social customs of his age. Women became some of his most beloved followers, and some of the leaders in the early Church.[28]

He challenged the racism of his day by telling a story about a man he perceived as good and righteous—a Samaritan, one of the most hated people in that time.[29] This would be similar to telling a Klansman a story about a good and righteous African-American.

He challenged classism by associating and even dining with the lowlifes of society—the rejects, the prostitutes, the tax collectors, the outcasts, the sick, the lepers, and the untouchables, saying that they would enter the kingdom before the religious leaders of the day.[30] He pardoned the repentant thief on the cross, telling him that he would join Jesus in Paradise.[31]

Jesus, as well as Paul, brought liberal values to the idea

of marriage. A Jewish man and woman were supposed to marry and to have children. Jesus was single, and didn't fulfill the appropriate social and religious customs of his age. Paul clarified that it didn't matter if a person were single or married; each was to be valued.[32]

Jesus was against capital punishment, a position that is considered a liberal value. He forgave the woman caught in the act of adultery, and freed her, even though the religious law of his time proclaimed that she be stoned to death.[33]

Jesus rethought the idea of forgiveness and vengeance, clarifying that no longer should one seek revenge through an "eye for an eye"; nor should one forgive another only seven times, but rather seventy times seven.[34] From Leviticus in the Hebrew Scriptures to Romans in the New Testament, Christians and Jews have been told to never seek vengeance toward one another. "Vengeance is mine, sayeth the Lord, but you shall love your neighbor as yourself."[35] The Book of Romans tells us, "do not overcome evil with evil, but overcome evil with good. Therefore, if your enemy hungers, feed him."[36]

In many ways, Jesus was far more radical than are the most liberal members of Congress, asking us to act in a way that we often find impossible and impractical. He changed the way we were to think about the enemy. We are to make friends with our enemies, recognizing that if we do not do this, there will be trouble.[37] Jesus expanded our idea of the neighbor, telling us that we are to think of our enemy as our neighbor, and he added a new commandment: to love our neighbor as ourselves. This doesn't mean that we are naive about evil, but that we don't add fuel to the fires of hatred. Rather than demonizing and attacking the enemy, we should use diplomacy, which is far more in line with the values of Jesus.[38]

Jesus practiced nonviolent resistance to oppressive laws. He suggested that we love our enemies—feed them, clothe them, care for them, and "offer no resistance to the wicked." This turns the enemy into a friend. Jesus advocated nonviolence with the enemy using a subversive tactic that is often used in nonviolent resistance. If the person of his day were asked for his coat, he was to give the cloak as well. If he were asked to go one mile, he was to go two miles.[39]

Why is this nonviolent resistance? If a person in biblical times gave up his coat and cloak, he would be naked, thereby shaming the person who asked him. It wouldn't take long for the Romans to decide that this was embarrassing and not effective.

A Roman was allowed to ask his subject to carry a burden for one mile, but not for longer. If someone started to walk the second mile, the Roman would be breaking the law. It wouldn't take long for the Romans to stop asking, once they realized that they couldn't stop their subjects from walking that second mile.

Jesus and the prophets rethought the social structures that generally rewarded the rich and powerful and asked us instead to change our focus to the poor and the needy. The prophets asked for a compassionate nation, and Jesus asked for a compassionate people. Who do we particularly need to care about? Those people who could not give back to us, but who were in need of our care.

Jesus rode a donkey, not an elephant. Elephants were ridden by the rich ruling classes. Jesus didn't identify with the rich ruling classes, but with the people. He was with the people and for the people and of the people—a core value of both democracy and Christianity.

The Ethics of Jesus

Jesus asked us to go beyond the letter of the law to the spirit of the law. Christian values go beyond simple rules to difficult ethical questions.

When Jesus picked corn on the Sabbath, and healed on the Sabbath, the letter of the law said this was wrong.[40] He raised the ethical question—"Does this benefit or harm others?" If it benefits others, we may need to change the law.

Our country has many difficult ethical problems to consider. How are we to handle the ethical dilemma of abortion? How are we to handle terrorism and the proliferation of nuclear weapons? Should we make treaties with enemies? How do we deal with the increasing gun violence in our culture? What about the wide-ranging effects of a global economy? What should we do about climate change and health care and education? Is same-sex marriage a just decision in agreement with our Christian and democratic values? The Bible gives us no clear guides on many issues, except to be willing to confront ethical problems, guided by the Holy Spirit and the Law of Love.

The Holy Experiment

Could Christian values and politics be compatible? Is it possible to govern effectively using Christian values? At least at one point of our history, religious values were applied to create a democratic society called the Holy Experiment.

In 1681, William Penn received a land grant from James II of England to the land that became Pennsylvania, as well as the colonies of New Jersey and Delaware. Penn had been an Anglican, but became a Quaker in 1668. His Christian values and principles informed his decisions about how to govern the state, and for sixty years, he was successful.

He affirmed diversity, and set out to create a colony that was open to all. To achieve diversity, Penn began by recruiting settlers from Holland, England, Ireland, Wales, and Germany.

His new constitution promised full religious liberty to all. He said in his charter of "Laws, Concessions, and Agreements" that "no Men, nor number of Men upon Earth, hath Power or Authority to rule over Men's consciences in religious Matters."[41] He wanted a government that would be contrary to war, selfishness, cruelty, suspicion, treason, judicial murder, greed, envy and betrayal, persecution, imprisonment, torture, and intolerance that existed in so many governments.[42]

He believed in the abiding principles of truth, love and equality, and applied them equally to the King and to the Native Americans, as well as to the many citizens of the state.

He called it his "Holy Experiment" because, as Benjamin Trueblood said, "it was founded in love, built up on the principles which love dictates and carried forward in the faith which is inspired and sustained by love."[43]

He governed the colony with just rules, and opposed any economic oppression of the many by the few, including any oppression of the Native Americans. He laid out the city of Philadelphia at a place owned by the Native Americans, and, instead of forcibly taking their land as many other settlers did, he paid them for their land. Voltaire later wrote, this was "the only treaty between these people and the Native Americans that was . . . never broken."

When the Native Americans met with Penn, they found no guns and laid down their own.[44] He established political freedom, founded on the democratic principle of an election by the people, providing for an elected legislative assembly and a Council appointed by the Governor.

It was also a colony without an army, with only a small police force, and without war, for most of those years. It had few judges, but successfully settled disagreements through arbitration. Every country court had several Peacemakers or Arbitrators. They only turned to a court of law when all other methods of settling disputes had been tried. There were only two capital crimes—murder and treason—which was a departure from English law where even minor theft, such as stealing a loaf of bread, could be punishable by death.

Education was emphasized. Prisons were humane. There was only one witchcraft case during this time, which ended without a conviction, in contrast to the hysteria of the Salem witch trials of Massachusetts.[45]

The colony was socially progressive. Since it treated the Native Americans fairly, it sought to extend these equal and just rights to others. In 1688, one of the towns in Pennsylvania—Germantown—began to question whether owning slaves was consistent with Christian values. Their influence led to the abolitionist movement.

Pennsylvania became the most tolerant and most diverse state in the early years of America, establishing the concepts of democracy and freedom of religion that later became so important in the Declaration of Independence and the Constitution.

William Penn showed that Christian principles could be put into action for the effective governing of a state. His particular Christian values were based on religious freedom and on governing through respect and justice.

Vote the Golden Rule

Many of us bring together our practice of religion and democracy by voting the Golden Rule. What we want for ourselves, we are also willing to give to others. We vote for the rights of others that we would also want for ourselves. We give the same protections, care, and respect to others that we would want for ourselves.

What would Jesus be doing in our society? As the Prince of Peace, he would be questioning our wars, which kill millions of civilians and leave millions of children homeless and as orphans.

As the One who accepts and loves, he would be rebuilding homes, instead of blowing up abortion clinics in the name of God. He'd be caring for AIDS victims instead of limiting the rights of homosexuals. He'd be volunteering at soup kitchens rather than cutting food stamps. He'd be planting trees instead of strip-mining public lands or creating policies that allow pollution. He'd be working to take care of those who have trouble surviving in our society, rather than rewarding the rich.

He would continue to question authority, knowing that power and privilege can easily corrupt.

Democracy asks us to debate and discuss issues to find

the best solutions. It asks many of the same questions that Christianity asks:

> *What are the most important issues the government needs to address?*
>
> *What is the goal of a Good Society?*
>
> *What are the means to reach this goal?*
>
> *How do we bring justice and mercy into a society, and create a society in which all of us, together, work for the Good?*

Chapter Two

The Poor, the Needy, Widows, and Orphans

"The spirit of the Lord is on me, for he has anointed me to bring the good news to the afflicted. He has sent me to proclaim liberty to captives, sight to the blind, to let the oppressed go free, to proclaim a year of favour from the Lord."

Luke 4:18–19

This was Jesus' first mission statement. It is often called the Social Gospel, because it proclaims His intent to move people from captivity, oppression, and afflictions to freedom. This is not only spiritual freedom, but actualizing the Kingdom of God within the society. This is a challenging message.

Many believe we create a Christian nation because most of the citizens are Christians, go to church, and believe in Jesus Christ as the Son of God. But the Bible does not limit religion to belief systems but calls on us to help liberate others from the burdens and trials that we and others endure. It asks us to consider the "least of these" and to make public policy with those who live on the margins of society always in mind. This has tended to be Democratic Party policy, and almost every Democratic candidate and every Democratic Party Platform pays attention to the needs of the poor, oppressed, and the disenfranchised.

The Republican candidates and platforms, fairly consistently, favor the wealthy and say little about the poor.

Many of us in America do not know people who are poor or destitute. If we do, we might believe their problems are of their own making and God really does help those who help themselves. Many Americans have lived in such privilege that we turn our eyes away from the homeless, blame the ill for their disease, try to justify why some live in poverty, and claim God's blessing to explain why we're so comfortable.

Our country is powerful and rich. We easily envy power and wealth, and try to get it for ourselves, forgetting that Jesus and the prophets ask us to change our perspective, and to take the side of the poor—to care about those without means, those who need healing.

The Command for Compassion

There is much disagreement about exactly what we, as Christians, should be changing in our nation. The Bible tells us nothing about many of the issues that confront us in contemporary society—whether we should talk to or negotiate with terrorists, what our energy policies should be, what kind of health care or educational system we should have. But there is one area in which the entire Bible is absolutely clear—we are to help the poor, the needy, the brokenhearted, the oppressed. It is the greatest litmus test we can apply to any governmental policies. If we had to choose only one issue that addresses the place where Christian values and political policy clearly come together, it wouldn't be abortion, homosexuality, education, ecology, or employment, it would be where we stand in helping the poor and oppressed. We as Christians are called upon to allow the Light of Christ to shine on the brokenness that is at the core of the human condition, individually and socially, and to be part of God's redemptive work on earth. This is not just an individual command, but a command to nations.

In Isaiah, God scolds the leaders of nations, "Shame on you . . . you who make unjust laws and publish burdensome decrees, depriving the poor of justice, robbing the weakest of my people of their rights, despoiling the widow and plundering the orphan."[1] God promised that he would bring justice to them and that He would crush their oppressors.[2]

In the Psalms, we are warned not to lose our good sense in prosperity, and are warned of the danger of becoming over-awed with the rich and those who live in great splendor.[3] When over-awed, we give preferential treatment to the wealthy. It is possible that the great support for Donald Trump comes because many are agog at his wealth. They wish they, too, had billions to spend on houses and casinos, and to self-fund whatever it was they wished to do.

In Amos, God condemns the rich: "for crime after crime of Israel, I will grant them no reprieve because they sell the innocent for silver and the destitute for a pair of shoes. They grind the heads of the poor into the earth and thrust the humble out of their way."[4]

The Bible tells us God is a stronghold for the oppressed, and He will not desert them. He listens to the laments of the brokenhearted. He fills the starving, and rescues those in chains and misery from hard labor. He gives the hungry a home and blesses them with a bountiful harvest. God provides a refuge for the weak and seeks justice for the poor.[5]

The Kings and Judges of the Hebrew Scriptures were commanded to find ways to equalize that which was unequal. They had authority over the nation, and woe to them if they only honored the rich! The poor were given the right to glean the edges of the fields for food, so they would not starve in a land of plenty. A tithe was to be collected every third year for them. The rich were not to make a profit from the poor, nor cheat them of interest on a loan, nor treat them as slaves. There were special compensations for the poor so they would not appear before God empty-handed. In the year of Jubilee, the poor could return and claim their ancestral lands; the injustices of the past would be ended and they could start anew.[6]

Protestant theologian Karl Barth, in his *Church Dogmatics*, says the Christian community "explicitly accepts solidarity with the least of little ones . . . with those who are in obscurity and are not seen, with those who are pushed to the margin and perhaps the very outer margin of the life of human society, with fellow-creatures who temporarily at least, and perhaps permanently, are useless and insignificant and perhaps even burdensome and destructive . . . these men are recognized to be brothers of Jesus Christ . . .

and therefore the community confesses Jesus Christ Himself as finally the hungry, thirsty, naked, homeless, sick, imprisoned man. . . ."[7] As we do unto the least of these, we also do unto Christ.

Can We Agree on Helping the Poor?

When setting out to write this book, I had presumed that this was one issue where we could find agreement among Christians. I was wrong. Although there are more than 2,000 verses in the Bible about the need for individuals and nations to help the poor and the oppressed, there is a powerful group of conservative Republican Christians that does not believe the Bible on this issue. They believe individuals and churches are asked to help the poor, if they so desire, but not nations. They believe charitable giving should only come from those who wish to give.

I must admit I was shocked to learn this. After all, this idea is coming from conservatives and fundamentalists who say they take the Bible literally. I started to question several of my colleagues who were conservative Republican Christians about this issue in order to understand it more clearly. I promised not to use their names in this book if they would clarify this issue for me.

I was told, by one conservative Christian, "We are called to help, not to force others to help or to use our mob power to steal from those who do not want to help." As a result of this theology, government programs are cut by Republicans whenever possible. Health care for the poor is de-funded. Getting an education or getting medicine or being able to

buy or rent a house becomes costlier because the government won't help. Another Republican Christian saw the liberal Democrats as giving far too many handouts, and said
the government shouldn't be in that business, even though
the Bible tells us that leaders and rulers and nations have
an obligation to give justice and to remove oppressive burdens. In his view, conservatives believe that "the church,
not the government, should be involved with helping and
caring for the poor."

I e-mailed him back, asking who the church is most apt
to help. Certainly they are most apt to help fellow Christians. Where does that leave the immigrant who has just
received citizenship but has few resources? Or the Muslim,
who lives in a poor community? What about the workers
who have been hurt by financial scandals when the CEOs
made millions of dollars? What about the drastic needs
that come from communities hit by a hurricane and left
with billions of dollars in damage? Or from the tsunami
that has washed away hundreds of thousands of people and
hundreds of communities, leaving needs far beyond what
one church, or two or three, or even one denomination, can
handle?

I asked, "How much money do most churches have?
Do they have enough to rebuild homes, pay for job training, provide food and medicine and doctor appointments
for the family in need? Is there any church, even the most
wealthy, that can afford what is needed as a result of a catastrophe or difficult, unbearable situations?"

One of the Christians said we should not be forced to
give money to causes that we don't believe in. He is also
a pacifist, so he said he didn't want to fund war. I agree. I

don't either. But people who adhere to this reasoning might think, "I shouldn't have my tax dollars go to funding education, because I don't have any children and I'm finished with my own schooling." Others might think, "I shouldn't have to fund Medicare because I won't have to worry about my retirement for a few more years, and Mom and Dad are dead." Perhaps they believe, "I shouldn't have to fund the roads in Iowa, because I haven't driven on them for many years." When did we become so selfish we forgot about the common good? If we followed this policy, it would divide the nation into prideful interest groups with only their own selfish desires at heart.

Some Christians don't see the necessity of helping the poor because they believe that they must focus on their individual relationship with Christ. After hearing this idea a number of times, I asked one of my Republican Christian friends, who is a Baptist, if she agreed with this. She said she did not. She answered, "There are plenty of lost, lonely, and deserted people within our borders to keep both church and state busy, so I fear that the statement that churches should fix the problem is a veiled form of greed. I don't see that the churches are responding, and therefore our disenfranchised people will be out in the cold, literally, which is truly heartless."

She continued, "Of course, churches should be stepping up and out for our own faith, but that does not mean we should eliminate government assistance. I don't see how anyone in their right mind can think that churches can replace Medicaid, or take care of all our health needs, or education and job improvement programs. There is a huge difference between soup kitchens and shelters and the long-term needs of people with mental and physical disabilities." This friend had been a Republican. She changed to the Democratic Party in 2008 partly because of the Republican stance on these issues (and partly because of the first edition of this book).

Another friend reflected, "I don't see any Republican governors refusing assistance when their state is in trouble." New Orleans and New Jersey received millions in assistance after hurricanes. California received help after their forest fires. Ebola and Zika outbreaks were handled quickly with government assistance to alert the public and to contain the diseases. An exception to this occurred when the governor of Michigan refused to ask for government assistance for the health hazards caused by poisonous water in Flint, Michigan. The U.S. government had to suggest and even beg to come in and assist the residents of Flint, many of whom were black and poor, and all of whom were victims of Governor Rick Snyder's merciless policies. "Nor are there any Republican members of Congress who have turned down their Social Security or refused their excellent health insurance. What they do for themselves they should consider doing for others."

After hearing from the many Republicans who do not agree with my friend, I wondered if I had misread my Bible. Perhaps I was wrong. Perhaps the Bible was only talking to individuals. I soon found more than 500 passages addressing nations. I reread the book of Jeremiah, the prophet appointed by God to talk to the nations. God said, "I brought you to a country of plenty to enjoy its produce and good things; but when you entered you defiled my country and made my heritage loathsome."[8] There are many loathsome acts which the nation did: "The very skirts of your robe are stained with the blood of the poor."[9] "There are wicked men among my people . . . they set traps and they catch human beings. Like a cage full of birds so are their houses full of loot; they have grown rich and powerful because of it, they are fat, they are sleek, . . . they have no respect for rights, for orphans' rights, and yet they succeeded! They have not upheld the cause of the needy. Shall I fail to punish this, Yahweh demands, or on such a nation to exact vengeance."[10] God tells the nation they must "treat one another fairly . . . not exploit the stranger, the orphan and the widow . . . not shed innocent blood."[11] He scolds the nation and its leaders for having "eyes and heart for nothing but your own interests, for shedding innocent blood and perpetrating violence and oppression."[12] The Democrats have a far better record at addressing these commands.

And What About the Stranger?

One of the most challenging issues confronting our country revolves around immigration. There are about 11–12 million undocumented workers in our country. About 50% of these come from Mexico. There are also hundreds of thousands of foreign travelers, sojourners, students from other countries, and refugees who come to our country for short or long periods of time, who are not "like us" but who have different skin color, cultures, dress, languages, and ways of approaching their daily lives. In theological language,

these people are sometimes called "The Other" and are objectified, dismissed, rejected, and told to go back to their
own country and their own people.

With regard to the stranger, some people act on the principle "Nothing human is foreign to me," while others seem
to be saying, "Nothing foreign is human to me."

The Bible recognizes the difficulties immigrants confront and asks us to respond with compassion. There are
more than one hundred verses in the Bible about how we
need to treat the stranger. The Bible put the needs of the
stranger along with the needs of the orphans and widows,
and told the Israelites that special care needed to be given.
They were told, "You must not oppress foreigners,"[13] you
must "Love the stranger as yourself," and you must not
"deny justice to the foreigner."[14]

Why are we asked to be so kind to strangers when they
seem on the surface to be a threat to the prevailing culture?
Historically, immigrants to any country were often brought
in to fill the need for cheap labor and to take the difficult
jobs that other people didn't want. They often came to escape economic hardships in their own country or to escape
war, famine, drug violence, threats, danger, or religious
persecution. Our Statue of Liberty asks us to take in the
tired, the poor, the huddled masses yearning to breathe
free.[15] The immigrants were often rejected, abused, and
forced to live in unsafe conditions, and had little legal
recourse.

The word *Hebrew* means "to cross over" or, said another
way, "to be a border crosser." Hebrews were almost always
strangers in a strange land. Sometimes the prevailing culture welcomed them, and sometimes it oppressed them.

Jesus was a sojourner, a stranger in a strange land, who was accepted by some but rejected and killed by others.

We are told to care for the "least of these," which means we are asked to feed and clothe and care for the stranger in the same way we would do for our family or our friends. The individuals and nations that don't do this are cursed. "Cursed is the one who perverts the justice to the stranger, the fatherless, and widowed."[16]

What policies and actions might result from our understanding and care for the immigrant? The Democratic and Republican stances on this issue show a clear division about how to treat the immigrant. All the Republican candidates, in one way or another, want to get rid of some, if not most, of these people.

Donald Trump's position is the most extreme. He would deport 11 to 12 million undocumented immigrants, which would be expensive and impractical. Trump would build a wall between Mexico and the U.S. (to block the arriving Mexicans, who make up only about 50% of illegal immigrants) even though the cost of the wall would be prohibitive. Trump would ban all Muslims from entering the United States and favor Christian immigrants to come into this country—although it seems that this would not apply to Mexicans, many of whom are Christians. He would not allow any Syrian or Middle Eastern refugees into the U.S. and would send the millions of Syrian refugees who have escaped from their violent country back to face further violence and perhaps to face starvation or death.

This negative attitude toward immigrants is a somewhat odd stance for a person who has married two immigrant women who were not born in the United States, who are not "culturally" American, and who did not become citizens until some years after the marriages. Trump has also employed hundreds of illegal immigrants at low wages, some working seven days a week. Obviously, he found them useful for himself.

The policies of Ted Cruz are similar to Trump's, and Marco Rubio's are only slightly more moderate—which again is unusual since both Cruz and Rubio are the children of immigrants. It just keeps getting, as Alice in Wonderland would say, "curiouser and curiouser."

John Kasich, who seems to me to be the most reasonable of the Republican candidates, says, "The symbol of the United States should not be barbed wire but the Statue of Liberty." Jeb Bush seems to recognize that many Mexican immigrants come to the United States with good intentions, which he sometimes calls "an act of love." This attitude has been criticized and ridiculed by Donald Trump.

Both Sanders and Clinton see immigration as a matter of compassion and security, and believe that when immigrants are properly vetted, there should be a path into the United States. That could be through green cards, through naturalization, and through citizenship.

Democrats would pass the "The Dream Act." The Dream Act says that children under 16 who were born in the United States, or who came to the United States with their illegal immigrant parents, should not be taken away from their parents or deported, but should be allowed to pursue a path to citizenship and to join the military, go to college, and become responsible citizens. Under current law the children can stay in the United States, but often the illegal immigrant parents must leave, abandoning their children. The Democrats do not consider this to be an example of family values.

There is a Celtic rune that expresses a Christian attitude toward "The Other":

> *I saw a stranger yestreen,*
> *I put food in the eating place*
> *drink in the drinking place*
> *music in the listening place,*
> *and in the sacred name of the Triune*
> *he blessed myself and my house*
> *my cattle and my dear ones,*
> *and the lark said in her song:*
> *often, often, often*
> *goes the Christ in the stranger's guise.*[17]

What Is the Human Condition?

If we are commanded to help the oppressed, we need to know who the oppressed are and why they're oppressed. Is it their own doing, or part of the wages of sin, or does oppression come from the rich and the powerful and the social structures that support the privileged?

To understand oppression, a number of theologians begin by looking at the human condition and by looking at the wages of sin. What is wrong with us? Why is there inequality and oppression? Why did Jesus come to save us? What, and how much, needs saving? Does our Fallen Nature, which is explained by the story of Adam and Eve, express why life has to be this difficult? What can be done to bring us back to the blessings of the Kingdom?

There are many interpretations of the Fall of Adam and Eve and what that Fall means for us. Some say it's a story about the fall from obedience to disobedience, from innocence to corruption, from unity to separation. An interpretation that is particularly meaningful to me comes from Protestant theologian Paul Tillich. He points out when Adam and Eve were in the Garden of Eden, everything was in harmony and in unity. They were in harmony with each other, in harmony with the Garden, in harmony with the animals, and in harmony with God. They walked in the cool of the evening with God. Obedience was not a problem. They had what they needed. It was, truly, Paradise.

The Fall, then, was the fall into disharmony, or what Tillich calls alienation or estrangement from God. The curse Adam and Eve received, and therefore we all receive, was alienation on every level. No longer would the plants easily grow when Adam tilled the soil. After the Fall, he worked by the sweat of his brow. No longer were Adam and Eve in harmony with each other. He dominated her, and yet she couldn't escape her desire for him. No longer were they in harmony with God. They were exiled from the Garden, where they had once walked so easily and closely with God. Immediately after the Fall came the violence of brother against brother, when Cain killed Abel. Then came disharmony in families, disharmony as societies began to form. There was violence over territory, violence over imposing one law over another, disobedience both relationally and socially. On every level, we were no longer free, complete, fulfilled, and joyful.

With the coming of Christ, we are given the opportunity

to move back into harmony with God. Our alienation and separation are overcome. The atonement brings us back into at-one-ment with God, through Christ. We are moved to express our regained freedom and joy by allowing Christ to work in our lives and by responding to others, as he responded to all of us.

Every part of our lives, and therefore every part of our society, can be touched by Christ—if we work toward allowing it to be. In fact, many Christians would say when the Holy Spirit works in our lives, we are continually and naturally moved into compassionate action with everyone around us—in our relationships with others, in our relationships with our neighborhoods, our cities, our states, our country, as well as globally. Christ is not limited. In an ever-expanding circle of life, we are called into the national and international arena, to express our faith in our world, to create justice, and to bring mercy.

Fighting Oppression Within and Without

Oppression happens individually, relationally, socially, and politically. Individually, we are in bondage. We are burdened and weighed down. This can be expressed in many ways. We might feel restless, as if we can find no peace within ourselves. Everything irritates us. We are impatient; we are afraid. We feel hopeless, unloved, uncared for. We are in a state of separation. We feel abandoned and cannot get connected. We are having trouble finding our way.

Salvation begins on the individual level. In my own experience, I began to find peace through daily reading of the Bible and other spiritual works. I began to feel connected to something bigger than myself and felt a Presence that could guide me and comfort me. I found a particularly helpful Bible verse to be: "Seek ye first the Kingdom of God, and all these things will be yours as well."[18] I began to feel, unless I found inner freedom and peace, I would continue to have trouble relating to the world and contributing to the world.

As I moved my faith into relationship, I struggled with pride and envy. I competed with others. I was jealous of everyone who had more than I did, or who seemed to have an easier life. After some years, I was able (with God's help) to see competitors as colleagues and begin relating easily to them. I began to find freedom as I entered more actively into a religious community. As a student at Colorado College, I began to attend Bible studies with the Navigators, a conservative Christian group.

Later, my Quaker community, both locally and internationally, nurtured me into moving my faith into the world. Quakers believe when we pray, meditate, and wait and listen to the Holy Spirit, we will naturally be moved into social action.

For each of us, that social action will take different forms—whether to visit the prisons, to feed the homeless, to help educate others, to help the jobless learn skills and find jobs, to build homes for others, to start recycling centers, to plant trees, to care for animals, to work for equality, to change the laws of our land to better help others—the list is, of course, endless.

For many of us, there is a point in our spiritual journey when we realize we need to make changes in our larger social world in order to help the oppressed. Oppression can come from oppressive organizations, laws, social structures, financial institutions, or governments. We might find we can't help the outcasts and those left behind because an oppressive government has declared our interference illegal. We can't help the prisoners who are tortured or executed, because we'll be imprisoned ourselves. We watch the innocent victims of oppressive governments and of war, and realize we can no longer work individually, but need to do something to address the root of the problem at the political level.

Working for God's Kingdom

A number of Christian denominations interpret the work of Jesus as being political and social work, not just work for the individual soul. This is true among the mainline and more liberal Christian churches, which have tended to be more attentive to the poor and needy. Increasingly, this has been a concern of the more conservative churches as well. In 2005, the National Evangelical Conference called for "greater Christian involvement in society including: poverty, human rights and justice." In a paper titled "For the Health of the Nation: An Evangelical Call to Civic Responsibility," which is the paper put out by the National Association of Evangelicals, there is a list of a number of specific issues Evangelicals are called to address: "disaster relief, refugee resettlement, and the fights against AIDS/HIV, human rights abuses, slavery, sexual trafficking, and prison rape." It goes on to list the "protection and well-being of families and children, of the poor, the sick, the disabled, and the unborn, for the persecuted and oppressed, and of the rest of the created order."

The paper recognized we are called to work for God's kingdom,[19] which would be a kingdom marked by "justice, peace, forgiveness, restoration and healing for all." We are to "demonstrate God's love for all, by crossing racial, ethnic, economic, and national boundaries."

Liberal denominations probably would add to this list, by clarifying that we are to work for gender equality and to show God's love for homosexuals as well. Who is to address these problems? Democrats would say individuals, churches, and the nations. In the Democratic Platform for 2008 and 2012, the Platform contains around fifteen pages about the need for the government to also address the poor and the needy. Who are these people? According to the Democrats, they are workers including women who have trouble supporting their families because they do not receive equal pay for equal work. They are veterans who return from war, physically and mentally wounded, who need health care and other forms of therapy. They are victims of disasters; some of these disasters come as a result of pollutants and climate change. They are Native Americans, Blacks, Hispanics, immigrants, widows, the aged, battered women and children, LGBT youth and adults. They include victims of hate crimes, the unemployed who are trying to keep their homes and their families together, and many who battle with health issues. The oppressed include those who are discriminated against because of race, creed, religion, age, class, gender, and sexual orientation.

Many families are oppressed because they have children they can't care for but have no access to contraception. The oppressed are victims of human trafficking, as well as those who are denied the right to vote and those whose unions are being dismantled so they no longer have a voice.

The Democrats have a long record of caring about the middle class and the 15% of our country who live in poverty. However, there is virtually nothing about discrimination and the poor in the Republican Platforms in 2008 or 2012. The Republican concern is for the wealthier among us. They want to make sure that everyone is enabled to "have a chance to own, invest, build, and prosper."[20] Rick Santorum, former senator and presidential candidate, was asked if the Republican Party cares about the poor. He responded, "I'm not sure we do."[21] Many Republican actions confirm this—blocking a bill to raise the minimum wage, cutting food stamps, voting "no" to the Fair Pay Act, denying low income and poor women access to basic health care; the list goes on and on.

Liberation Theology: Transforming the World

We take the Gospel into society and ask, "What can the Gospel tell us about the best choices to make when we're creating laws and public policy? What does it mean to be a Christian in society? How do we best express our Christian values and our faith in public?"

In 1968, a number of Catholic priests, bishops, and laypeople met at Medellín, northwest of Bogotá, Colombia, and began questioning how to be more effective in their work with the poor in Latin America and South America. They recognized that the poor are often kept in poverty by social, religious, and political structures. They looked at ways the government, the Church, and the wealthy colluded to make the rich richer, and the poor poorer. The participants wanted to understand how they could be effective in changing social conditions that would also change the abject poverty and misery of millions of lives.

In 1973, Gustavo Gutiérrez wrote a book called *A Theology of Liberation*. Liberation theology is a practical theology, addressing the practices necessary to transform the world into a more just, caring place. Gutiérrez believes "communion with the Lord inescapably means a Christian life centered around a concrete and creative commitment of service to others."[22] This theology seeks to build "a world where every [one], no matter what his race, religion, or nationality, can live a fully human life, freed from servitude imposed on him by other men or by natural forces over which he has not sufficient control."[23] It seeks a society "based upon justice, respect for the rights of others, and human fellowship."[24] Pope Francis, who is from Argentina, comes out of this Liberation Theology background, which explains his great care for the poor and the underprivileged.

Liberation theology critiques government policies that keep the poor in their state of poverty. It is a social and political theology standing up to oppressive regimes and oppressive laws.

What Have We Done to Help the Poor?

We know what we're asked to do. How have we done as a nation? It depends on the year. The Democrats have been known as the party that responds to the oppressed, and they have a good history of making social change that helps the lower rungs of our society.

When our country was in the depths of the Depression, President Franklin Delano Roosevelt created the New Deal, a set of social programs that addressed unemployment, unfair distribution of income, and corruption in government. It offered relief, recovery, and reform. People were put back to work, cleaning up the national parks, building barracks for the military, providing programs for scholars and artists. The Republicans criticized the government for interfering, but the Democrats realized that the system wasn't working and needed help from the government.

During Roosevelt's presidency, a number of bills were passed to try to fix the problems. In 1935, the Social Security Act was passed. Then the Labor Relations Act, which broke up monopolies, outlawed price fixing, and gave labor the right to organize. These rights had been taken away during previous Republican administrations and have been threatened currently by Republican governors and Republican members of Congress.

During Lyndon B. Johnson's administration, the Civil Rights Act of 1964 was passed, giving greater protection to those suffering from discrimination and racist policies. The Voting Rights Act also was passed, abolishing the poll tax, which had interfered with the voting rights of the poor, particularly blacks. Both of these laws have been challenged by a Republican Congress and by a conservative-leaning Supreme Court. The Food Stamp Act was passed in 1964; the Economic Act of 1964 created the Community Action Program, Job Corps, and Volunteers in Service to America (VISTA). The Social Security Act of 1965 created Medicare and Medicaid, two social services that have also been challenged by a Republican Congress.

President Obama signed the Lilly Ledbetter Fair Pay

Act in 2009, restoring protection against pay discrimination. Obama also signed the Fair Pay Act of Congress in 2013 to prohibit discrimination in the payment of wages on account of sex, race, or national origin. He has tried to pass a number of bills that would help veterans and the unemployed, regulate the excesses of Wall Street, address gun violence, and end discrimination. Most have been vetoed by a Republican Congress.

Recently, new obstacles to voting rights have been implemented. There is a drastic difference between the Democrat and Republican toward voting, because the Republicans are concerned about voter fraud and the Democrats are concerned about the disenfranchised. Democrats want to make sure that voting is accessible. They are concerned about the many stringent requirements that Republicans are adding to eliminate early voting and eliminate many polling places, which forces many voters to stand in lines for two to eight hours to vote.

Martin Luther King Jr. said we can judge a nation not by how it coddles the rich, but by how it cares for the poor. Our country is definitely coddling the rich.

Helping the Super-Rich

During his presidency, Bill Clinton raised taxes on the wealthiest taxpayers, and expanded tax breaks for the working poor. George W. Bush did the opposite. He created more tax cuts during his presidency, but most of the tax cuts benefited people with incomes in the top 10 percent, and more than 15 percent of the tax cuts went to the top 0.1 percent who make up the super-rich.[25]

The taxpayers with the highest incomes pay the same percentage of income, Medicare, and Social Security taxes as those making $50,000 to $200,000. President Obama has tried to return to the tax rates under the Clinton administration, believing that the current taxes are not fair. Hillary Clinton and Bernie Sanders recognize the inequity of tax laws and want to expand taxes on the top one percent of incomes of people and corporations who have unfairly benefited from Wall Street bailouts and tax cuts.

We might say, "More power to the rich!" We might find no problem with this because we too hope to be wealthy. Or we believe being super-rich shows how much God loves us. Or we might believe the wealth of the rich will trickle down to us. Not true. Not at all. The yearly incomes of the super-rich have increased, and there is greater and greater inequality in the difference between the super-rich and the poor. There have been increases in the investments and returns of the wealthy, but the lower 90 percent of the taxpayers aren't getting any. Sanders and Clinton both would address the excesses of Wall Street as well as corporations and the many tax laws that favor the rich.

The middle class and wealthy often criticize the poor for being welfare recipients, but we all get welfare. Road repairs allow us to easily move from one place to another. Street lights protect our neighborhoods. Schools, libraries, museums, all supported by our taxes, enrich our lives. There are government subsidies for airports, airlines, and trains. If we're middle class or wealthy, we receive subsidies for our travel on airlines or trains by taking it off our taxes as business expenses. We take trips and deduct our hotels and meals and travel fares because the trip, including the golf game, the fishing excursion, and the Las Vegas show, are enjoyed with business associates. Since the rich and middle class receive all these subsidies, how can they cut food stamps for the poor and bus routes which make it possible for the poor to get to work? This isn't "communism," it's "community."

Some of the wealthiest Americans, such as Warren E. Buffett, George Soros, and Ted Turner, all Democrats, are concerned this concentration of wealth can turn our society into an aristocracy. Ted Turner said, "The growing gap between the super rich and the middle class in the USA and around the world disturbs me. . . . More alarmingly, the five richest people in the world are worth more than the combined annual net worth of 63 countries. Extreme economic disparity works against the interests of freedom and democracy. I don't believe the richest Americans need more tax breaks. . . . Believe me, they don't need it."[26]

At the Democratic Convention in 2004, Barack Obama recognized that positive change can only be achieved through our ability to empathize with those in need: "I am my brother's keeper, I am my sister's keeper. . . . If there is a child on the south side of Chicago who can't read, that matters to me, even if it's not my child. If there's a senior citizen somewhere who can't pay for her prescription and has to choose between medicine and the rent, that makes my life poorer, even if it's not my grandmother. If there's an Arab American family being rounded up without benefit of an attorney or due process, that threatens my civil liberties. . . . I am my brother's keeper."

How many of us have relatives or friends who are struggling because their health care needs aren't taken care of? How many of us know someone who has to decide between food and rent or medicine? Just ask around, and chances are you know someone who is struggling with this issue. One of my friends, now 73, receives $1,260 a month from her husband's Social Security, which she started receiving after his death. She pays $270 a month for her low-income apartment. She does not receive food stamps because she was deemed to receive too much money from Social Security to qualify. Her groceries for the month are about $400. She has a car that is now twenty years old, which she needs for doctor appointments and occasional visits to friends because she lives near Los Angeles where there is not adequate bus service or other forms of public transportation. She cannot afford to do the usual maintenance on her car. Her car insurance is $50 and gas is $100. Her medical expenses, even with Medicare, are $300 a month. Her phone, cable, computer, and Internet costs are $120 per month. And, of course, she has to buy any number of supplies just to live, such as paper for her printer, oil for her car, toothpaste and deodorant, dish detergent, cleanser, etc. She can never afford to eat out. If she goes on a date, she hopes the man pays. Once in a great while, she goes to a movie; when she does, it's an afternoon matinee to save money. She has not been able to work for some years because of the pain and problems that come from two hip replacements and two knee replacements from arthritis. She lives in almost constant terror, not knowing what will happen to her. Recently, she had to start selling the little jewelry she had, including the wedding ring from her husband, simply for living expenses. This would not be happening to her if she lived in most European countries, and even in some non-European countries. Any one of us reading this knows that there is no leeway for her monthly expenses or emergencies. There is no padding for her anywhere—not from savings, not from relatives, nor from children, since she has no children or living relatives who can help her.

Budget Cuts Show Our Priorities

The Bible says, "For wherever your treasure is, that is where your heart will be too."[27] We know what the government treasures by seeing who gets the money. We might say we can't afford to address the poor, or global warming, or education, or social services, but if all of Mr. Bush's tax cuts were repealed, our government would have enough revenue to take care of many of our social problems. Where is the heart of the Democrats? Their priorities are clear: Both Clinton and Sanders focus on campaign finance reform, climate change and energy, making college accessible to all, reforming the criminal justice system, preventing gun violence, healthcare, immigration reform, repairing and strengthening the infrastructure, working for equality, overcoming discrimination, racial justice, preserving Social Security and Medicare, helping veterans, and preserving voting rights.

The Most Rev. Frank Griswold, former presiding bishop of the Episcopal Church, USA, said there are three questions that should be asked about any budget: "Is the budget compassionate? Does the budget strive to serve the human family, both at home and around the world? Does the budget serve the common good?"[28]

Expanding Our Neighborly View

When Jesus was asked which was the greatest of the Ten Commandments, he said there were only two that would encompass all others: "Love the Lord your God with all your heart, mind and soul, and your neighbor as yourself."

But who is my neighbor? Jesus challenged us to expand our view of whom we are directed to care for. It is easy for us to be kind to the neighbor next door, the person we like—the one who goes to our church, who is of our own race, and even the same gender. Of course, that person is our neighbor, and as people in community, we should be neighborly toward each other.

In the Good Samaritan story, Jesus expanded our concept of our neighbor. Jesus deliberately chose, as his main character, a Samaritan, who was a member of one of the most hated cultures in biblical times. When a man had been robbed and left for dead on the side of the road, everyone walked by—the priest, the Levite, the people known as the "good religious people." Who helped the wounded man? A Samaritan, who paid for the injured man's healing and thus showed himself to be the true neighbor.

Protestant theologian Karl Barth, quoting Kierkegaard in his book *The Epistle to the Romans*, says, "But the neighbor is—everyman. A man is not thy neighbor because he differs from others, or because in his difference he in some way resembles them. A neighbor is the man who is like unto thee before God. And his likeness belongs to a man unconditionally."[29]

Who is your neighbor? Those whom you like and even

those you don't like. It is a radical Gospel, and that is what Christianity is—simply radical! It stretches us, and asks us to think differently, to think against our human nature, which says, "No way! That's not what it means! I wouldn't lift a finger to help that man!" We are asked to think of those we hate as our neighbors, and to set social policy that deals compassionately, and justly, with them.

That means we are asked, as a society, to look out for the dispossessed and the needy, whoever they may be: the Muslim who has been jailed, perhaps for being at the wrong place at the wrong time; the terrorist—yes, even the terrorist who is being treated inhumanely, whether at Guantánamo or shot and bleeding on the street, or a victim of his own inhumane act; the homosexual who may be the victim of hate crimes; the hurt and the helpless; the person who can't afford health care; the battered woman; the abortion doctor who is reviled and even shot at for doing a job that is legal in the United States. Make your list of the people you hate. Those are the people you're asked to feed and clothe, and to whom you are to show fair treatment, justice, and mercy.

These are the people we are asked to help in our governmental policies as well. What we want for ourselves—compassion and rights—we must also allow and protect for others.

Chapter Three

Beautiful Savior, King of Creation

*"Yahweh God took the man and settled him in the
Garden of Eden to cultivate and take care of it."*
Genesis 2:15

At the beginning of the Bible, God is introduced as the
Creator of the natural universe. The earth is described as
beautiful. He calls it Good. For thirty-one verses, the Bible
tells us of the wonders of God's creation. The Glory of Creation is recounted again in the Psalms, in Job, in Proverbs
8, in John 1, in Colossians, and in Revelation.[1]

Both the Apostles' Creed and the Nicene Creed begin
with the image of God the Creator: "I believe in God the Father Almighty, Creator of Heaven and Earth" and "I believe
in One God, the Father Almighty, Creator of Heaven and
Earth, and of all things visible and invisible." After God created the world, He committed what some might think was
a foolish act. He commanded Adam and Eve to "be fruitful,
and multiply, and replenish the earth and subdue it: and
have dominion over . . . every living thing that moveth upon

the earth."[2] This verse from the King James translation has set environmental policies for centuries. Many people on our planet have interpreted these words to mean we can do with the earth what we please. It's ours, to serve us. We can take from it what we need and more. We can rape and exploit the earth if we want to.

But what does this really mean? There are two important words used in these verses. An entire theology is created out of how we understand and interpret the words "subdue" and "dominion." If we misinterpret these words from their original meaning, we misinterpret our theology and proceed to act in error. As a result, we cause irreparable damage to God's creation.

The word "subdue" in the Hebrew is *kadash* (sometimes spelled *kavash*). The word implies a hierarchical relationship, in which human beings are given control and power over the earth.[3]

Radah (or the Hebrew root, "rdh") is the word for "dominion." It means "to rule as God rules" or "the right and responsibility to rule, to govern the rest of creation."[4]

When put into context, it seems that dominion and subjugation were understood as "a call for restraint in the rule over material and animate creation, for self-limitation, and for harmony both with fellow human beings and the rest of the world."[5]

Genesis 1:28, says theologian Walter Brueggemann, "emancipates man and sets him over nature and makes him responsible for 'nature' entrusted to him. Nothing in this text supports the contention that it authorizes the kind of action which has issued in our current ecological crisis."[6]

If we are to rule as God rules, we can ask, "Does God oppress or liberate? Does God imprison or release? Does God beautify the earth, or destroy it?"[7]

Before the Fall, we could have dominion over the earth because we had kept our relationship to God. After the Fall, we were estranged from God, estranged from each other, and estranged from the earth. God could no longer trust us. With the eating of the forbidden fruit, we had surpassed our authority. If we had been allowed to live forever, we would be a rival to God.[8]

The Fall tells us that we cannot be trusted to obey, to be good stewards, to be responsible over what God has given us. We only have to look at many of the ecological catastrophes on our earth to know that harmony and responsibility have been lost. All that had been so wonderful and perfect in the Garden was marred, destroyed, taken away from Adam and Eve. No longer were they masters, but slaves. No longer were they in relationship with God, but cut off and separated.

From Dominion Theology to Dependence Theology

Christians who believe we are to have dominion over the earth and subdue it often have a "pre-Fall" theology, which we can find in Genesis 1. But there is another theology that calls us to recognize our deep connection with nature. This theology appears in Genesis 2 and in most of the rest of the Bible. In Genesis 2, Adam, the human being, is made out of topsoil. The word *Adamah* is sometimes translated as "earth person" or, we might say, the "earthling was made out of the earth" or the "human was made from humus."[9] Adam was created much like plants and animals were created. The divine breath blown into the nostrils of Adam is the same breath by which the animals live and breathe. Here the role of the human is to "serve"[10] or "to till," and this is the work of slaves serving their masters and humans serving God.[11] Adam is told to cultivate and to take care of the garden. Here the idea is not of lordship, but of servanthood.[12] It is a theology of dependence rather than domination.

Which theology do we choose? Domination or service? Theodore Hiebert, professor of Old Testament at McCormick Theological Seminary, says both theologies "capture the paradox of human existence." On the one hand, we believe ourselves to be powerful and in control, a view expressed in Genesis 1, which has led to our ability to destroy the human race entirely through our misuse of our resources.[13] "On the other hand, we know ourselves as humans, as does Genesis 2, to be only a single species in a large and complex web of life we do not entirely understand and can never really control. . . . Our only hope of survival in fact, is in recognizing our dependence on this web of life and adapting our behavior."[14] "Special attention to the dependence theology of Genesis 2 is important . . . because our greatest temptation as individuals and as a race is to think more highly of ourselves than we ought to think. Indeed, it may not be an oversimplification to say it is just such a proud and self-centered perspective that has allowed us to exploit nature for our ends and has brought upon us the ecological crisis we now face."[15]

Seeing Ourselves in Relationship

If we look at nature, we can see we are part of a system that interacts with animals and with the earth. If we see creation as relationship—relationship with each other, relationship with the earth, relationship with God—we might feel love and awe for God's work, which leads us to live more responsibly with the earth.[16]

After we were told to have dominion over the earth, that commandment began to be clarified: In Chapter 2 of Genesis, we are told to cultivate and take care of the garden. We are given the ultimate responsibility—to work the garden, to dress it, to keep it as it was created—to keep it good.

Throughout the Bible, there are other commands given to us about how to treat God's creation:

We are to guard and protect the animals. Noah was asked to save two of every species, so they wouldn't become extinct.[17]

In Proverbs and in Deuteronomy, we are told to show compassion to animals.[18] "If you see your brother's donkey or ox fall over on the road, you must not disregard it, but must help your brother get it on its feet again."[19]

When we work with animals, we are to treat them properly. "Thou shalt not plow with an ox and an ass together."[20] Plowing with animals of two different sizes would be a hardship to them.

We're told to protect the trees that bear fruit. "If, when attacking a town, you have to besiege it for a long time before you capture it, you must not destroy its trees by taking the axe to them; eat their fruit but do not cut them down."[21]

God gave us a legacy and a command—to take care of the earth. What have we done in return? We've contaminated the lakes, rivers, and streams. We've polluted our skies. We've scarred the land through strip-mining. We've allowed thousands of species to become extinct. We've bombed and raped millions of acres of land. We've changed the climate of the earth, causing droughts, floods, hurricanes, and global warming.

Many of these problems are coming from developed countries and developing countries. It is often the rich minority that consumes the most resources and causes most of the pollution, especially by increasing technology. Our acid rain floats across the border to do harm to Canada. The industrial pollution from Germany has killed some of the forests of Norway. The nuclear accident at Chernobyl continues to cause problems not only in Ukraine, but also in surrounding areas.

But it's not only the rich countries that are to blame. There are also the slash-and-burn policies of Brazil and Indonesia, and clear-burning in Africa for farming, as well as overfishing in remote Pacific islands. Our footprints on the earth have not made this earth better. We have not been good stewards. We have not cared enough.

The Cosmic and Mystical Christ

Every religious interpretation of Creation expresses the glory of God found in creation. Those Christians who believe in "Intelligent Design," or in Creationism, can see God's genius in His creation. Others, who acknowledge Evolution, see the wonder of the creative process set in motion by God's divine spark, which continues to evolve into beauty and wonder.

There is a theology called Creation Theology, which believes we have been given an Original Blessing with the creation of human beings and with the creation of the earth. This theology sees our lack of caring and our unwillingness to be good stewards as an affront to the Holy Spirit and to the Mystical or Cosmic Christ, who exists within creation.

This way of seeing Christ and the Holy Spirit in creation is not new. Many saints and other Christian writers have said that their spiritual journey has moved them toward learning to see God in everything, including nature. God is both immanent—within the earth and within all of us—and transcendent—beyond the earth and beyond us. This is not pantheism (worshipping nature), but a way of seeing the Divine within, about, and around us.

Meister Eckhart said, "Everything that is, is bathed in God, is enveloped by God, who is round-about us all, enveloping us. . . ."

Hildegard of Bingen said, "All of creation is a song of praise to God." Matthew Fox, who has a number of books and articles about this theology, calls it "a way of seeing the world sacramentally."[22]

This viewpoint sees nature as more than a "thing" God has given us to play with, work with, and use as we want. It is closer to the idea that the Spirit of God infuses all creation with Its Presence, and is without limits in our world.[23]

As a Christian, I understand the Spirit is within me, not just somewhere "out there." Julian of Norwich says, "We are in God and God, whom we do not see, is in us."

Quakers say, "There is that of God in everyone"; sometimes they call it "The Christ Within, the Seed, the Light Within." Others speak of a sense of the Presence.

Although most Christians probably agree that the Holy Spirit can exist within people, some may find it more difficult to believe that the Holy Spirit can also be within other physical matter.

Yet, every time we take Holy Communion, we are attesting to this fact. Some churches believe that when the bread and wine are blessed before the Lord's Supper, they *become* Christ. Matter has become Spirit.

Catholic theologian Pierre Teilhard de Chardin, in *Hymn of the Universe*, goes a step further, believing that Christ penetrated all of matter when he became incarnate in a physical life. He believes that Christ is not limited by the physical body; the love and delight that God has for creation, the love that God has for matter, causes matter to have a spiritual dimension. He says, "To be pure of heart means to love God above all things and at the same time to see him everywhere in all things."[24]

According to Matthew Fox, the concept of sin in Creation Theology consists of "injuring creation and doing harm to its balance and harmoniousness, turning what is beautiful into what is ugly."[25]

In Creation Theology, all is potentially redeemed by Christ. As Revelation tells us, there is, and will be, a New Heaven and a New Earth.

Whether we see God and Christ *within* creation, or creation as a gift from God to us, it is still blessed. It is still declared as Good.

Poet Elizabeth Barrett Browning wrote, "Earth's crammed with heaven, and every common bush afire with God; And only he who sees takes off his shoes; the rest sit round it and pluck blackberries." God is here and everywhere, if we only but see.

Becoming Aware of the Sickness

We can't resolve any problems if we deny them. With any sickness, we begin the cure by admitting that the sickness exists. Then we decide to do something about it.

In order to understand the state of the sickness of our environment, it might be helpful to use an analogy of a sick person who is trying to get well.

In 2004, my sister was diagnosed with ALS (the affliction also known as "Lou Gehrig's Disease"). Often, when people first get sick, there are a variety of reactions. In the case of my sister, the doctors didn't take it seriously for more than a year. They ignored it, saying, "It's nothing! You'll feel better soon. It's just a little cold or flu. You're just a little under the weather!"

At some point, sometimes when it's too late, it becomes clear to everyone that this person is very ill. In some cases, the seriousness of the disease makes people want to distance themselves from the person who is sick. Doctors may not have time to see her, or may only suggest some stopgap measures that do very little to treat the disease. In some cases, friends desert the person, not wanting to be too close to her, or not knowing what to do or how to help.

Others get realistic about the disease and begin to assemble their resources. People who knew my sister began to recommend doctors, and tried to think of everything they could possibly do to help her get better. They sent her articles about various medicines, various treatments, about people with the same illness. Because my sister was a Christian, there were many prayer groups formed to pray for her. In my sister's case, a Christian friend had a Christian friend who knew a Christian doctor who had also been diagnosed with ALS and then rediagnosed with Lyme disease. He went on a regimen that healed him. Because of his miraculous recovery, he began to focus on studying this disease and then opened a clinic to treat it. My sister was retested, and it began to seem that she had Lyme disease, not ALS. But further tests showed that it was in fact ALS, which is fatal.

Those of us who wanted her to get better knew the value of her life—to herself; to her siblings and her relatives who treasured her good spirit; to her coworkers, who adored her and respected her work as a microbiologist; to her church community, which had rejoiced in her musical talents for well over twenty years; and to her Bible study group, which was supported by her kindness. Her health was of concern not just to her, but to all of us who loved her. Although we all went to great lengths to save her, she died in 2006, a month after the first edition of this book was published.

This same analogy holds for how we think about the

earth. Many people don't believe there's a problem. They believe there is no proof of climate change, of an increasingly contaminated water supply, of low food production, of pollution. They don't see the sickness, and continue to carry out policies that lead to further sickness. They discount the problem. It doesn't matter to them how many scientists identify and define earth's sickness; it just doesn't seem important enough to them.

Some know there's a problem but aren't worried, because it doesn't seem as if it will affect them personally. They believe that any major problems won't come to fruition for at least another fifty years, and by then they'll be dead.

Others see the sickness, but think the wonders of current technology will solve all the problems when the problems get bad enough. They believe that somehow, something, from somewhere, will come to the rescue. They don't think about how long it takes and how much money it takes to develop workable technologies. It's a bit like telling a dying person, "Don't worry. In another ten years, there'll be a cure for your disease. You just have to wait a bit!"

There are those Christians who believe these environmental problems are evidence that the end of the world is nigh, and they say, "Bring it on!" They see no reason to do anything about the environment because the problem will be over and done with soon; at least it will be for Christians, when we're all raptured up to what is, we hope, a more environmentally pure heaven. Armageddon is on its way, along with the Second Coming of Christ. They figure the worse it gets, the sooner we'll see Jesus.

Some see the sickness, and see it doesn't just hurt one or two people, but affects billions all over the earth. They recognize that we have the power to kill others, either quickly or slowly, by ignorant or repressive environmental policies. They recognize that we are hurting our neighbor, whether it's the person nearby, or the people in the next town, in a neighboring country, or far across the sea in another land. We forget we are to be Good Samaritans in all things, no matter where our neighbor may live. Both Clinton and Sanders consider climate change to be one of the foremost challenges we must address and solve.

Defining the Problem

It is difficult to solve a problem until we define it. What is the sickness of our planet? Most scientists can agree on these points.

Water tables are dropping. Because of droughts and misuse of land and water in China, India, and the United States, water tables are falling and wells are running dry. When water levels fall, the level of grain production also falls, which, in turn, leads to famine. This leads to higher prices for grain, which leads to farmers overworking the soil in an effort to get more crops, which leads to soil erosion and desertification of land that was once rich and fertile.

When food and water are scarce, violence often occurs between villages and nations as they fight over these necessities. When the water level goes down, clean water is difficult or impossible to find. A third of all the people on earth do not have access to clean water. Contaminated water leads to diarrhea, cholera, malaria, and sickness and death, especially in children.

When we have less water, corporations seize the opportunity to take control of the scarce water supplies and begin selling water. They privatize water, depriving people of their access to water and leading to increased poverty.

Some economists see water as the oil of the future, and predict that countries with enough fresh water will market it to countries where water is in short supply. Although on the surface it might seem that moving clean water would be helpful for water shortages, much of this water is marketed as bottled water, which only the middle class and wealthy can afford.[26]

Sometimes governments manipulate the agricultural harvest. Much of America's wheat land is kept fallow each year. It may be possible to feed everyone in the world, but when farmers are paid subsidies not to grow certain crops, it further contributes to the problem of hunger.

Temperatures are rising. Increasing temperatures are affecting our food supply. Some might say that we shouldn't be concerned just because it's a little warmer this year. Not true. We should be very concerned. The International Rice Research Institute in the Philippines and the U.S. Department of Agriculture indicate that for each 1.8-degree Fahrenheit rise in temperature during the growing season, we can expect a 10 percent decline in fields of wheat, rice, and corn. The hottest year on record was 2015. Temperatures rose 1.8 degrees Fahrenheit.

The Intergovernmental Panel on Climate Change, made of up 1,500 scientists organized by the United Nations, projects that average temperatures will rise more than 10 degrees Fahrenheit during this century. If we don't do something about climate change, millions of people will die as a result of drought and famine, and of the violence that comes from the struggle for scarce resources.

Food prices are rising. The scarcity of food leads to rising food prices. The resulting rise in grain prices will destabilize governments in the many countries that have very little money but must import a substantial amount of grain.

Food and water are being polluted. Not only does our food supply become scarce because of our environmental policies, but many of those policies make the food we have unfit to eat. Acid rain and pesticides also make fish and other food products inedible.[27]

Earth in the Balance

Al Gore, former senator, vice president, and presidential candidate, wrote a book in the early 1990s titled *Earth in the Balance: Ecology and the Human Spirit.* Later, he won an Academy Award for the documentary based on this book, which is called *An Inconvenient Truth.* Gore's book provides some of the best scientific and religious thinking on the environment. It approaches environmental and energy issues from the viewpoint of Scripture, ethics, morality, and spirituality, while also bringing together sound scientific information.

Gore looks at our confusion about environmental issues by also looking at our confusion, as Christians, about how we are to relate to the earth. Christians have been of two minds about this throughout history. For some, we are separate from the earth, and independent of the earth. What we do, in our own little moral universes, has little bearing on what happens on the earth. Our thoughts are about eternity, and about being heavenly minded. Of course, some Christians are so heavenly minded that they're no earthly good.

Other Christians see this differently. They believe we are entrusted with the earth by God. As good, responsible stewards, we recognize that what we do has consequences and, just as we wouldn't destroy a church or kill our neighbors, neither would we desecrate the earth, which was given to us as a gift. We are integrally connected to the earth, not separated from it.

Consider these miraculous statistics. The percentage of water in our bodies is the same as the percentage of water on the earth.[28] The percentage of salt in our bodies is approximately the same as the percentage of salt in the oceans of the world.[29] We are unified with the earth physically, as well as spiritually.

In fact, we are so connected that what each of us does in our own part of the planet affects the other side of the world. Famines, floods, fires, hurricanes, or any natural or unnatural catastrophes can change our individual lives, and they can also change our society.

Gore recounts a number of these connections in his book, but one that particularly impressed me occurred in the 1930s—the Dust Bowl years.

In the 1920s, the mechanization of the tractor, the combine, the one-way plow, and the truck led to unwise land use. Farmers, as well as other experts, mistakenly believed that repeatedly plowing the land until it was smooth and pulverized made it better able to absorb and hold rainwater. For a few years this worked well. There were record crops,

and the early signs of the danger of wind erosion were ignored.[30] Then, in 1932, strong winds began to blow, taking
away some of the topsoil. Then came rain, and flooding,
which further eroded the soil. When this was followed by
a dry winter and spring, the big dust storms began taking
more of the topsoil, leading to a drought. In 1934, Secretary
of the Interior Harold Ickes told the people of Oklahoma
to leave their homes. By that time, only 15 percent of the
acreage of Texas and Oklahoma was useable.

Dirt and dust were everywhere. The earth was barren.
Emergency hospitals were set up to treat "dust pneumonia"
and other respiratory diseases caused by inhaling the dust.
The dust and dirt blew all over the West, and even to the
Atlantic Ocean. As a result, farmers could not make a living
in their own states. They were without work and lost all of
their land. So what did they do? They started moving into
other states, such as California, which could not absorb this
vast migration of people. This led to unemployment and
hunger. There were food riots. There were long bread lines.
Finally, legislation was passed to help those who suffered,
requiring millions of dollars of government money, specifically from Franklin Roosevelt's New Deal legislation.[31]
Who suffered? Our entire society. Our lack of environmental policies can cause consequences not just for the earth
and not just for individuals, but these policies affect all of
society.

Gore clarifies in his book that this is not just a scientific
problem, but a moral problem as well. Many Christians feel
a moral obligation to respond when we hear that mankind
is slashing and burning one football field's worth of rain
forest every second, and destroying half of the living spe-

cies on earth in the space of a single lifetime. Over 376,000 children under the age of five die from starvation every day because of failures of crops and failures of our politics. Yet still we pump millions of tons of pollutants into our environment, threatening the earth's climatic balance.[32] We continue to build gas-guzzling trucks and SUVs and cars, which benefit the oil companies in the short run but don't serve the many of us who ask for better mileage.

Where do we see God? In a dead bird? In sick animals? In polluted water? In polluted skies that cause sickness for us and our children?

In December 1989, Pope John Paul II addressed his "brothers and sisters in the Catholic church, in order to remind them of their serious obligation to care for all of creation. . . . Respect for life and the dignity of the human person extends also to the rest of creation, which is called to join man in praising God."[33] Are we creating a world that praises all creation? Are we becoming good stewards? Or don't we care?

Learning to Care

The lack of response to the environment by Republicans has been an ongoing problem under Ronald Reagan, George H. W. Bush, and George W. Bush; Republicans in Congress continue to veto bills that will address these problems. When a number of people protested Mr. Reagan's policies, which were going to destroy hundreds of redwood trees, he shrugged off their concerns, saying, "If you've seen one redwood tree, you've seen them all."

When many people protested drilling for oil in the Arctic National Wildlife Refuge, even former Secretary of the Interior James Watt, known for his pro-development stands, agreed that the region was too sensitive for drilling. Yet the push for drilling continues in spite of the dangers. The Republicans wanted to build the Keystone XL Pipeline in order to bring more oil from Canada into the United States, but the Democrats were concerned about the Pipeline because a by-product of the oil refining process, petroleum coke or "pet coke," poses a health threat due to the high sulfur and carbon waste. There is a threat from the dust, which can cause coughing, wheezing, and shortness of breath, as well as other respiratory conditions. There are other threats from the Pipeline; the original Keystone Pipeline had twelve oil spills in the first year and over thirty spills overall.[34] It also posed a threat to the water tables, and this led Nebraska to refuse to bring the Pipeline into its state. The bill approving the Pipeline was passed by the Senate and the House, but Obama vetoed the bill and the Congress did not have the votes to overturn his veto. The Democrats recognize that polluting and climate change may disproportionately affect the poor. They are committed to environmental justice.[35]

Former head of the Environmental Protection Agency, Republican Christine Todd Whitman, recounts a number of other ways in which her own party has continued to discount environmental concerns.

In her book *It's My Party Too*, she quotes Vice President Dick Cheney, who said, "Conservation may be a sign of personal virtue, but it is not a sufficient basis for a sound, comprehensive energy policy."[36] If conservation—care for the environment—is not a basis, then what is?

Some Republicans handle these problems by denying there are any problems at all. Donald Trump says climate change is a hoax. Ted Cruz and Ben Carson also don't believe that climate change is real or that some of it is manmade. Marco Rubio and Jeb Bush say it's real but they have no plans to do anything about it.

Climate change is very low on the Republican priority list. In fact, some candidates don't even address it.

Hillary Clinton and Bernie Sanders see climate change as one of the top priorities to address because it affects so many other issues: the economy, jobs, the future we leave to our children. Clinton wants to make America the world's clean energy superpower. She says, "I won't let anyone take us backward, deny our economy the benefits of harnessing a clean energy future, or force our children to endure the catastrophe that would result from unchecked climate change."[37]

Bernie Sanders connects climate change with campaign finance. He is particularly concerned about the money poured into presidential campaigns, because billionaires such as the Koch brothers have gotten their money through fossil fuels and have a vested interest in making sure that the government continues to focus on oil and coal rather than alternative energy sources.

The refusal of Congress to deal with global warming has been costly. We have already suffered many of the effects, and can only expect to have more tragedies in the future. Climatologists have studied the effect of global warming on our oceans and see a connection between the rising water temperatures and the intensity of hurricanes of the last thirty years. Ruth Gorski Curry, research specialist from

the Woods Hole Oceanographic Institution, says, "As carbon dioxide levels climb to levels unprecedented in the last
400,000 years, the planet is warming, its ice is melting, and
evaporation/precipitation patterns are changing. . . . Most
climate simulations agree that greenhouse warming will
enhance the frequency and intensity of hurricanes and ty-
phoons in the coming century."[38] The number of category 4
and 5 hurricanes, such as Hurricanes Katrina and Rita and
Sandy, has almost doubled since the 1970s. Scientists see
this pattern connected to the steady increase in water temperatures, which have risen 1 degree Fahrenheit in the last
thirty years. Although scientists don't see evidence of more
hurricanes as a result of global warming, they see evidence
that the warming of the oceans is producing hurricanes of
greater intensity, which in turn have created greater rainfall
from the hurricanes.

Our unwillingness to be visionary, to plan for the future,
to care about our environment, and to take care of problems
before they get out of control is now costing us billions of
dollars to rebuild cities ravaged by Hurricanes Katrina and
Rita and Sandy.

Denial becomes more and more expensive. After Hurricane Katrina in 2005, George W. Bush said on an ABC
television interview, "I don't think anyone anticipated the
breach of the levees." But that is not true. He was repeatedly warned about this problem but refused to take any action. In 2004, the *New Orleans Times-Picayune* said, "For
the first time in 37 years, federal budget cuts have all but
stopped major work on the New Orleans area's east bank
hurricane levees, a complex network of concrete walls,
metal gates and giant earthen berms that won't be finished

for at least another decade." The article predicted that if there were a strong hurricane, the area would "fill up with the waters of the lake, leaving those unable to evacuate with little option but to cluster on rooftops—terrain they would have to share with hungry rats, fire ants, snakes, and perhaps alligators. The water itself would become a festering stew of sewage, gasoline, refinery chemicals, and debris."

The tragedy from Hurricane Katrina did not take us by surprise. It was a tragedy waiting to happen. George W. Bush's repeated refusal to fund the drainage systems and the levees magnified the disaster. He repeatedly slashed funding requests from the Army Corps of Engineers. When the Corps asked for $26.9 million, Mr. Bush asked Congress for $3.9 million, which delayed seven contracts that would have improved the levees that hold back Lake Pontchartrain. When the Southeast Louisiana Urban Flood Control Project asked for $62.5 million, the White House proposed $10.5 million. When former Republican Congressman Michael Parker protested the lack of proper funding, he was forced out as head of the Army Corps of Engineers. Former Louisiana Senator John Breaux, a pro-Bush Democrat, said, "All of us said, 'Look, build it or you're going to have all of Jefferson Parish underwater.' And they didn't, and now all of Jefferson Parish is underwater."[39]

The flooding of Manhattan from Hurricane Sandy had been predicted for years. In 2009, the New York City Panel on Climate Change predicted, "In the coming decades, our coastal City will most likely face more rapidly rising sea levels and warmer temperatures, as well as potentially more droughts and floods, which will all have impacts on New York City's infrastructure."[40] It is predicted, "whether in 50 or 100 or 200 years, there's a good chance that New York City will sink beneath the sea." Former Governor Andrew Cuomo made global warming a subject for public debate and suggested building a levee in New York Harbor. But nothing has yet been done.

What Would the Democrats Do?

The Democrats recognize that our environmental policies also affect the economy and the family. "The health of our families, the strength of our economy, and the well-being of our world all depend upon a clean environment."[41]

The Democrats are committed to "promoting new technologies that create good jobs and improve our world." They want to "strengthen the Clean Air Act by controlling all of the top pollutants and offering new flexibility to industries that commit to cleaning up within that framework." This means reducing mercury emissions, smog, acid rain, and water pollution that originate from factories, large corporate farms, storm-water runoff, and sewer overflows. It also means cleaning up the polluted sites, such as the nuclear waste dump in Nevada. The Democrats also want companies that lease lands to restore them to their original state when the lease runs out.

The Democrats want to preserve wildlife, and protect the lands and rivers used by hunters and fishermen. Because they recognize that the global environment impacts the American environment, and vice versa, they would work with others overseas to address these concerns, including the concerns of climate change and global warming.

Democrats recognize that our environmental policy and our energy policy must work hand in hand. We must gain independence from foreign oil.

Our lack of a strong environmental policy doesn't just pollute our country, nor does it just pollute other countries. Our dependence on these resources affects the state of the world. Our economy depends on oil controlled by some of the world's most repressive regimes. We are often silent about the practices of some governments because we depend on oil they control.

The Democrats have specific specific action statements:

Harness the natural world for energy—sun, wind, water, geothermal and biomass sources, and our crops.

Give tax credits to those whose companies use more energy-efficient methods.

Create energy-efficient vehicles, including hybrid cars and hydrogen cars.

Improve fuel standards.

Seek more diverse sources of oil, including areas already under exploration, such as Mexico, Russia, Canada, and Africa.

The Republicans want to put more focus on nuclear energy and coal by building more nuclear energy plants and coal plants and to use more hydraulic fracturing, which has been blamed for some of the sinkholes and water pollution. The Democrats put more focus on alternative sources. Republicans take a market-based approach. They want the free market and the public preference to determine policy. They would like to have more oil and natural gas exploration on federally owned lands. Democrats are concerned about the rolling back of public health safeguards, and they believe that jobs can be better created through promoting clean air and clean water and a healthy environment.

What's the Effect?

Energy policies also affect us on a far more profound level. The countries that are rich in natural resources, particularly oil, hold us hostage. Their regimes become increasingly more oppressive to their citizens as governmental leaders get richer, live more lavishly, and rule with an iron fist. These oil-rich countries become more dependent on only one industry. Those who work for that industry get the benefits. Those who don't become poorer. When the citizens try to protest, they're killed; all of the weapons and all of the power lie in the hands of the small group that controls this one resource.

Ultimately, this leads to war. It's no accident that our last three wars have involved oil-rich countries—Kuwait, Afghanistan, and Iraq—or that Russia's annexation of Crimea was partly to have a port for oil export. This is where many of the problems are, and they exist on many levels. We get involved in the repressive regimes that have oil—invading and occupying their land—but don't get involved in the genocide in countries that have little oil and don't serve our own national interests.

Through this long chain of connections, our policies perpetuate the social injustices in our own country and in other countries in the world. The rich get richer, because they're associated with oil. The poor get poorer, because the resource is scarce and they have to pay more for it.

There is a Native American saying that has been borrowed by many religions—we are to recognize that our actions will affect the seven generations that follow us. If we were to think of our actions in connection with their long-term consequences to future generations, we might have drastically different policies.

We have been tempted, in our dominion over the earth, to play the despot rather than the benevolent king. St. Basil, Bishop of Caesarea, created a prayer in the fourth century to acknowledge, and expand, our sense of stewardship: "O God, enlarge within us the sense of fellowship with all living things, our brothers the animals to Whom Thou gavest the earth as Their home in common with us. We remember with shame that in the past we have exercised the high dominion of man with ruthless cruelty, so that the voice of the earth, which should have gone up to Thee in song, has been a groan of travail. May we realize that they live not alone for us, but for themselves and for Thee. That they too love the sweetness of life."

Chapter Four

The Ethical Dilemma of Abortion

"Make your view heard . . . on behalf of
all the unwanted; . . . defend the cause
of the poor and the wretched."

Proverbs 31:8–9

There is one thing we probably can all agree on: a loving marriage with happy and healthy children is a great blessing.

But life doesn't always work out this way. Women marry and are abused, battered, threatened, and killed. Many children are neglected, and live in unsafe and unhealthy environments. In other periods of history and other parts of the world today, the women and children would not have any recourse. They would be forced to stay in an unhappy family situation. In some religions, the woman would be told that under no circumstances should she divorce. She might be allowed to leave, but certainly not start a new life. Matthew, Mark, and Luke are very clear: "everyone who divorces his wife . . . makes her an adulteress; and anyone who marries a divorced woman commits adultery."[1]

87

I don't hear either Christian Democrats or Christian Republicans arguing about divorce anymore. It seems to be a secular law most religions accept as part of our national laws, even if they don't accept it for their own church members. But in order to understand various Christian attitudes toward abortion, it might help to understand attitudes toward divorce and how they exist side by side with secular laws.

When I was twenty-two, and shortly after I had become a born-again Christian, I married. Naive about relationships, filled with romantic illusions, I married a man I didn't know well. Even before the wedding, I felt a growing uncertainty about this relationship, but I didn't know how to end it, nor was I convinced that it wouldn't work. In my religious innocence, I figured God would make everything right. I felt obliged to trust and have faith.

Within days, I realized I had married an emotionally abusive man. He was controlling, picky, and critical. He stole without remorse—nothing big, but our little apartment was furnished with chairs and tables he took from the Army base where he worked. This behavior created a deep conflict within me. On the one hand, as a fundamentalist Christian, I figured I was stuck for life. But, because I was a deeply spiritual person, something seemed wrong with this interpretation.

Several times he threatened my life. He didn't hold a gun to my head, but he would tell me, "I might kill you some day. I wonder how I'll do it. There's a gun in my closet, but I might do it while you sleep by smothering you with a pillow."

As a Fundamentalist, I kept telling myself, "I just have to be more loving." But it didn't matter how loving I was.

Clearly this man did not love, cherish, or respect me. In fact, I knew, deep inside, that he didn't even like me! I soon realized I did not have the strength to live in fear without its having severe consequences in many different levels of my life.

In one of my prayers about what to do about this, I told God I didn't understand. I said, "If I'm not allowed to get divorced, then marriage to an abusive man is the only sin that can't be forgiven. I could kill someone, serve my time, and come back into society as a changed person and go on to try to live a happy life. But if I marry someone who is abusive, I can't ask forgiveness and start again. I am stuck. And my only options are insanity, suicide, getting killed, or getting a divorce and suffering the condemnation of my Christian community."

As I thought further about the situation, I realized I was becoming more and more depressed and immobilized. I had recently finished graduate school. I had studied hard for a career, and knew that I had contributions to make. But I would be unable to make them in this situation.

I realized the fundamentalist interpretation of the Bible allowed me to leave him, but not to get a divorce. Therefore, neither of us would ever be able to marry again, until one of us died. Since I was only twenty-three, I didn't see death for either of us as a possibility unless he carried out his threat to kill me. Nor did I understand how a mistake at twenty-two should determine the happiness or unhappiness of my entire life.

After more struggle and reflection, I realized this view of a God uncaring and uncompassionate did not reveal the loving God I had begun to know. I also realized that it was imperative I leave the marriage, since it would be unfair to bring a child into this situation.

Because no birth control method could be trusted 100 percent, there was no way I could be sure I wouldn't get pregnant. I feared for my physical life and my emotional life if I continued to have any ongoing relationship with this man. I knew that when I left, I had to make sure he wouldn't know where I had gone.

I did leave, and eventually got a divorce. I told all of our mutual friends to write to me through my parents, who would forward the letters. I couldn't trust these well-meaning friends to keep my location a secret.

Although I felt that my religion would not support my decision to divorce, my country's laws did. I was allowed to get a divorce and start life again, as a wiser, more careful person.

I was offered a teaching position at a Southern Baptist college, where I revealed to the dean and the president (but not to students or other faculty members) that I was divorced, thinking that they might not accept me onto the faculty. Although they did accept me (and I later learned that both of them also got divorced), I kept my divorce secret for a number of years, for fear of being censured by religious people. Keeping the secret kept me from finding some emotional resolution to my divorce and from getting on with my life. Seventeen years later I remarried, and found the love and spirituality that I so desired in a relationship.

As the years went on, most churches began to acknowledge divorce as a solution in difficult circumstances.

Soon after my divorce, I started looking at other churches that weren't as fundamentalist and legalistic. I did further study of divorce, and began to understand that divorce had originally been forbidden as a way of protecting women from a man who could simply say "I divorce you" three times and throw her out on the streets. I also saw how these same verses could be used to control women. When the verses against divorce are combined with the verses in Ephesians 5 about the woman being submissive to a husband, they could justify the oppression of the wife—including beating her, not allowing her to see anyone or do anything without the husband's permission, and keeping her tied to him with a very tight rope. I have met women who are in unhappy and oppressive marriages and whose misery shows through in their faces and in every movement they make. They are in complete bondage to husbands who cannot, or will not, change.

I began to realize, experientially, an overly legalistic and literal interpretation of the Bible can get in the way of one's relationship with a loving God and the guidance of the Holy Spirit.

From this experience, I began to see how very flawed our decisions can be and how very difficult and complex many relationship issues are. I recognized my church and my country might disagree with each other about how to resolve certain issues. Some churches would not recognize my right to a divorce. My country did.

The Right to Life and Liberty

There are issues in the United States in which the pursuit of life, liberty, and happiness and the rights of the individual conflict with certain religious beliefs. American citizens struggle with how much the government should be interfering in our lives. Should the government be legislating individual morality? If so, does that mean that police will be peering into our bedrooms to see what we're doing? Will they be checking to see what books we're reading, who we associate with, what marches or parades we take part in, and where we're traveling? Some extremists would like to peer into our private domain, but make it clear we are not to peer into their domain of the banks and the boardrooms.

The government struggles with determining which issues are of interest to the state, and which are not. Government regulates many areas that might seem to be personal decisions—such as the seat belt laws, child restraints in the car, the helmet laws, food labeling laws, zoning issues, no-smoking laws, and so on. We accept these laws because not doing so would cause negative economic consequences to our society. When people don't use seat belts or helmets or proper child restraints, police drag out the battered and the dead from accidents. This leads to more money spent on medical needs as well as civil services that could have been prevented.

We try to understand how far to go with legislating what seem to be personal freedom issues. Should we legislate sex, since the cost of sexually transmitted diseases, pregnancy, and abortions can also be a drain on society? And if so, do we legislate against a person who has sexual relations with anyone other than a monogamous, healthy spouse? Do we go too far when we peer into everyone's sexual practices to decide who is moral and who is legal? Many issues divide us as we struggle to understand which issues are of interest to a nation, and at what point our government interferes too much with our individual freedoms.

The Hot-Button Issues

One of the most divisive issues in our country is that of abortion rights. What is the government's interest in these rights? Why is there so much disagreement, among legislators and among Christians, about what to do about this?

There is not one verse in the Bible that mentions abortion. Many Christians who are against any abortion rights look to certain verses, but the verses can be interpreted in different ways. Some who try to take a literal interpretation of a verse may have to ignore the spirit of other verses. Some who take an overall spiritual or theological view of certain Scriptures may have to ignore the strong implications of other passages.

Is it possible for us to find some clarity about these issues, so we aren't constantly dealing with seeming contradictions? Have we, perhaps, misinterpreted some Scripture, in the same way we formed new interpretations about what the Bible had to say about slavery and women's rights? Will these issues continue to divide us for many years to come, or might we find some common ground that will help us resolve them?

A Woman's Right to Choose

Conservative Christians are against abortion, but so is everyone else. No one chooses to have an abortion because it's fun, or easy, or a good form of birth control; if we could make abortion unnecessary, we would all be grateful. The issue is not about abortion, but about who has control over a woman's body. Democrats tend to be pro-choice because they believe this is a personal and individual choice for the woman whose body is carrying the fetus. The difficult choice of having an abortion, according to the Democrats, is best made with the counsel of a spiritual leader, or a doctor, or her partner, or the advice of wise friends. Clinton and Sanders are both pro-choice. Both parties, however, have members who are pro-choice and pro-life.

Conservative Christians have taken the strongest stand against abortion. There is a concerted effort by many conservative Christians to back appointment of U.S. Supreme Court judges who will overturn *Roe v. Wade* and make laws to close down clinics that provide abortion and women's health care. Republicans have tried to de-fund Planned Parenthood clinics, even saying they would shut down the government if the government does not de-fund it. Republicans object to Planned Parenthood because they perform abortion services, even though this is only a small percentage of their work. For many low-income and poor women, this is the only health care they get. Planned Parenthood provides screenings for breast cancer, diabetes, cholesterol and high blood pressure; they provide birth control, support to pregnant women, flu vaccines, and basic healthcare.

Many Democrats see this closing down of clinics, such as Planned Parenthood, as creating negative consequences for our society, leading to more unwanted children, a higher crime rate, and more women on welfare. It will take us back to the years of back-alley abortions, with more women dying from self-induced abortions and from botched abortions performed by incompetent doctors. The rich, of course, won't have to be too concerned because they'll be able to fly to another state or country for a safe abortion. If *Roe v. Wade* is overturned, the individual states will again have the right to make their own laws concerning abortion. This means, for example, that abortion might then be illegal in Texas but legal in California. Currently there are laws against transporting a minor across state lines for an abortion without the parent's permission. This law won't affect the adults who can drive across the state lines on their own, but it will affect the pregnant minor. As usual, the burden will fall on the poor.

Many Christians base their stand about abortion on the Scriptures. But what do they find in the Scriptures specifically against abortion? Nothing. Jesus never mentioned it. Nor did Paul. Nor did any of the prophets, nor any of the writers in the New Testament.

In the Hebrew Scriptures, there are several verses that are used to justify the stand against abortion, although none of them specifically mention abortion. They are, however, strong and clear passages about God's love for us, and protection of us, including the unborn.

They talk about how God has made us,[2] formed us in the womb,[3] called us before birth.[4] The Bible tells us we are not to question if a child is deformed or retarded or blind, deaf, or mute. We are not to question God about his children.[5] The child is the Lord's, not the mother's or the father's.

The Bible does not, however, tell us who is to control a woman's body when difficult ethical problems need to be resolved. The state? The national government? The doctors? A local pastor? The husband? The family?

The Bible tells us that God protects the pregnant woman, and is wrathful toward anyone who hits a pregnant woman.

However, there is a chapter that seems to contradict this idea. If somebody takes every verse in the Bible literally, they need to deal with the one verse in the Bible that seems to suggest abortion is acceptable in certain circumstances. In Numbers 5:11 there is a story about a husband who suspects his wife of being unfaithful. He takes her before the priests, whose job it is to prove whether or not she was unfaithful. There is nothing said about why the husband believes this to be true. Was she pregnant and did he suspect that this was not his baby? Had he caught her in bed with somebody else? Had he noticed suspicious behavior? Or was he simply suspicious for no reason? The priests test her faithfulness by giving her a bitter herb. If she was unfaithful, the herb would wither her womb and she would never be able to have children again. If she was unfaithful and was pregnant, naturally the herb would kill the fetus. If she wasn't unfaithful, the herb would not have any effect on her, although we might presume that, whether she was unfaithful or not, the bitter herb would damage her body.

If she was pregnant, then abortion would be considered legal in cases of unfaithfulness, because there would be an abortion as a result of this bitter herb.

There are no verses in the Bible about the kind of punishment the man would receive if the man was unfaithful.

We might question whether this is the beginning of a more loving marriage or an abusive and controlling marriage. If so, we recognize that there are a number of verses in the Hebrew Scriptures that justify this kind of control. Clearly, neither the husband nor the priest cared about the woman or the fetus. They only cared about the husband's honor or shame. I would never make a political decision based on these verses if I were pregnant. But some people have made political decisions based on verses that are even less clear than this one.

This kind of thinking makes many Democrats nervous, because it seems hypocritical and uncaring. Bernie Sanders calls this the height of hypocrisy, saying that Republicans want limited government except when it concerns the intrusiveness into the bedroom and into a woman's body. It also concerns the Democrats because so many Republicans seem to value the fetus above people killed by gun violence, above the lives of refugees and immigrants, above the poor, above the victims of war. This raises even more ethical problems. Without *Roe v. Wade*, there will be more unwanted pregnancies where the woman will be forced to bear that child, even in cases of rape or incest.

This causes more difficult ethical problems. If the mother is dying and she could be saved by abortion, some conservatives would say the doctors must not, ever, save the mother. They must allow her to die, and try to save the fetus. In this case, they make two moral decisions: First, it means they believe taking action that will result in a death (of the fetus) is worse than taking no action at all and allowing a death to happen (to the mother). Second, they believe this group of growing cells, whether still an embryo within the first few weeks or a fetus, has exactly the same rights to live as the mother, and in fact even more rights, whether or not it would be able to survive on its own outside the womb.

They believe even if the fetus is damaged in some way, or can't be carried to term, or would not live more than a few months after birth, abortion would still be considered wrong.

It is, of course, easy for some of us to decide what someone else should do. When problems in pregnancy become
personal, and there's danger to someone we love, how does
that change our ethical decisions?

Love Can Change Decisions

A few years ago, a good friend of mine, whom I'll call Jane,
was happily pregnant. She had married recently and was ea-
gerly anticipating a baby. Soon after she became pregnant,
the doctor told her there was something very wrong with
the fetus. The doctor couldn't diagnose it exactly, but suggested abortion. Since Jane and her husband were against
abortion, they prayed for a miracle. As the months went by,
the doctor became clearer about the problem. She told Jane
her baby would almost certainly die in the womb. Again,
the doctor recommended an abortion, since the pregnancy
was still in its early stages. Jane and her husband decided to
allow the process to take its course. Jane called several of us
to keep us informed about what was happening.

Jane's mother, who is a conservative evangelical Christian
and would never consider herself pro-choice, made a pro-
choice statement—"Whatever you decide, your father and
I support you." Since I'm pro-choice, I made a similar statement: "Whatever you decide, you have our support. But I
do have some questions that are important for you to think
about. Are you in danger by carrying this fetus? Could this
be a danger to your life? Could this lead to an inability to
have other children?" My husband, who is also pro-choice
and who works in medicine, mentioned to Jane, "It's very
dangerous for you to have dead matter in your body. If you

decide to carry the fetus until it dies, make sure the doctor supports this decision and will remove it immediately." If the doctor didn't support her decision, we suggested she get another doctor. My husband and I both admitted our concerns about her health, but put no pressure on her to get an abortion. This was her choice, but above all, we wanted her to be safe and to not harm her health. It was clear, from everything the doctor had said, that there was virtually no hope for this fetus to live.

After five months, during a checkup, the doctor discovered there was no longer a heartbeat. Instead of removing the fetus immediately, the doctor waited four days and sent her to an abortion clinic. Shortly after Jane returned from the clinic, she began bleeding and was then taken to the hospital, where she stayed for several days. Clearly, there was more danger than had been expected.

If *Roe v. Wade* had been overturned, Jane would not have had the freedom to choose whether or not to have an abortion. Because she wasn't the victim of rape or incest, and because it didn't seem that there was immediate danger to her health, she would not have had the freedom to choose to carry the fetus until it died. The law would have deemed there was not sufficient danger to her health to justify an abortion. Yet, in retrospect, there was serious danger.

Jane's story is filled with ethical dilemmas. At what point does one give up hope? How does one judge the danger, when no one can possibly know all the possible medical problems? Whose rights should take precedence in this situation—Jane's or those of the fetus? If Jane had been working full-time, what consequences would there be for her health and her job and her welfare, knowing she would not be able to bring the child to term? Who should make

the judgment about how to handle this difficult dilemma—
Jane or the government?

Jane's decision to stay the course deepened her spiritual
life. She and her husband felt close to God as they struggled
with the decision. She believes it strengthened her marriage. For her, there was clearly a positive spiritual side to
her decision, in spite of the dangers. And that's what pro-
choice is—allowing each person to make the choice as she
is so guided. I, personally, would not want Donald Trump
or Clarence Thomas or Ted Cruz, or the minister down the
street, or the person next door to be deciding Jane's fate.
I would want Jane to make an informed decision, perhaps
with the help of her family and her family doctor and her
pastor, or perhaps through prayer and meditation and
reflection.

Without *Roe v. Wade*, it would not be her decision, but
someone else's. Without *Roe v. Wade*, if someone is raped,
the fetus would not, under any circumstances, be aborted.
If a teenager were the victim of incest, she would have to
carry the fetus to term, even if the father would not allow
the baby to be put up for adoption, and even if the girl knew
the baby would be beaten and abused by her father as well.

Of course, not all unwanted pregnancies are this catastrophic. Some result from failure of birth control. Some
are caused by foolhardy behavior and passions unchecked.
There are those who would say these girls and women
should be punished, and even deserve to suffer for their behavior, although these same people rarely mention punish-
ing the man, who may just be "sowing his wild oats," or so
overcome with passion he couldn't help himself. Who suf-
fers? The mother and the child.

It isn't just teenagers who are getting pregnant. What are the married people to do if they can't afford another child? Are they to be celibate?

The Social Consequences of Abortion

Unwanted children present problems to society, and these lead to other ethical dilemmas. Has abortion increased or decreased certain social problems, such as crime? In the book *Freakonomics*, authors Steven D. Levitt and Stephen J. Dubner explored the ways in which unwanted children affect our society. They noticed crime had been at an all-time high until it began to fall in the early 1990s with a suddenness that surprised everyone.

The rapid decrease seemed unexplainable. They began to study what might have caused it. They looked at the aging of the population, tougher gun control laws, the increased number of police, a stronger economy. They discovered, after careful examination, that these factors had very little or no effect. Then they looked at the issue of abortion.

After 1973, a woman could have an abortion if she had an unwanted pregnancy. The authors wondered if this could have had an effect. To analyze this, they began by looking at other societies, such as Romania, where abortion was declared illegal in 1966. This had an immediate effect on the society. The birth rate doubled within one year, and as the unwanted children grew older, they did worse in every way: they tested lower in school, they had less success in the job market, and they were more likely to become criminals.[6]

Before 1973, there were several states that allowed abortion. In that year, *Roe v. Wade* made abortion legal throughout the United States. Justice Harry Blackmun wrote the majority opinion, clarifying the harm to the mother, and to society, that can result from denying women a choice. "Maternity, or additional offspring, may force upon the woman a distressful life and future. Psychological harm may be imminent. Mental and physical health may be taxed by childcare. There is also the distress, for all concerned, associated with the unwanted child, and there is the problem of bringing a child into a family already unable, psychologically and otherwise, to care for it."[7]

The authors go on to say, "The Supreme Court gave voice to what the mothers in Romania . . .—and elsewhere—had long known; when a woman does not want to have a child, she usually has good reason. She may be unmarried or in a bad marriage. She may consider herself too poor to raise a child. She may think her life is too unstable or unhappy, or she may think that her drinking or drug use will damage the baby's health. She may believe that she is too young or hasn't yet received enough education. . . . For any of a hundred reasons, she may feel that she cannot provide a home environment that is conducive to raising a healthy and productive child."[8]

The authors saw the most important impact from legalized abortion was the impact on crime. In the early 1990s, which would have been the time some of the unwanted children would have become rebellious teenagers starting on a life of crime, the rate of crime fell. And it continued to fall. "Legalized abortion led to less unwantedness; unwantedness leads to high crime; legalized abortion, therefore, led to less crime."[9]

The authors admit their research could lead to many reactions—disbelief, shock, revulsion, and objections. They rechecked their research by comparing how crime rates fell in the states that legalized abortion before *Roe v. Wade*. They looked again at Romania and the effect of abortion on its society. They looked to see if states with the highest abortion rate eventually had the lowest crime rate. They looked at studies in Australia and Canada to see if they also affirmed this link. They saw the negative ramifications in a society that forbids abortion. They reached the conclusion "when the government gives a woman the opportunity to make her own decision about abortion, she generally does a good job of figuring out if she is in a position to raise the baby well. If she decides she can't, she often chooses the abortion."[10] They were also aware of the moral ramifications: "One need not oppose abortion on moral or religious grounds to feel shaken by the notion of a private sadness being converted into a public good."[11]

What does this mean? They discovered, from a purely social viewpoint, the positive aspects of abortion outweighed the negative. Abortions helped society by leading to a lower crime rate; less cost for trying, convicting, sentencing, and housing criminals; and less cost to families, schools, and society for all the problems unwanted children bring.

Legal abortions reduce risk since abortion is not risky with women who go to a professional provider. Every year, 68,000 women die in countries where abortion is illegal. Making abortion illegal does not stop it. In fact, the abortion rate in countries where it is illegal such as Chile, Peru, Nigeria, and the Philippines is higher than in the United States. Here's another fascinating statistic: The abortion rate drops when Democrats are in Congress or the White House. The abortion rate in the U.S. was lower under Clinton and Obama than either Reagan or G. W. Bush. The abortion rate has dropped 13% since 2008. The abortion rate dropped or held steady every year for 20 consecutive years except briefly between 2005–2006, when the rate increased while both Houses of Congress and the White House were occupied by pro-life Republicans. These statistics tell us that electing pro-life politicians does not translate into lower rates of abortion, and electing pro-choice candidates does not increase the incidence of abortion. Access to improved contraception appears to be far more useful than abortion restrictions in reducing abortion rates. In fact, abortions declined in the Midwest where the number of abortion clinics increased.[12]

Abortion rates are lowest in Western Europe where abortion is legal and covered by national health insurance, and unwanted pregnancies are fewer. Belgium has the lowest abortion rate. Abortion is legal, and there is sex education that recommends abstinence, stresses responsibility, and also teaches teens how to use contraception.

If the Republicans outlaw abortion, what does this mean from an ethical viewpoint? If the Republicans are going to overturn *Roe v. Wade*, they will also need to pass bills, create programs, and legislate policies that will make up for the negative effects unwanted children can have upon society. If they're going to force women who can't afford children to have babies, they're going to have to put aside money for better prenatal care, better health care, better job training for the fathers and mothers who have another mouth to feed, better pay in the form of raising the minimum wage, better child care for the children when the parents are at work, better funding for schools—many of which are now drastically underfunded—better after-school programs for the children whose parents are working during those hours in order to pay for their children's pre-school, better housing so parents can better shelter their children, better educational programs for the children, and more jails, more policemen, and more judges to handle the increased crime rate in case all the other social programs don't work.

They will need to create better adoption programs, making sure that their fellow Christians do not adopt only healthy white babies, but also babies from other ethnic backgrounds, as well as crack babies, and other babies with mental or physical disabilities. Since the Republicans have never before made these issues a priority, there is no reason to think that they will do so now.

Although Republicans would like to see churches and charities take care of social problems, this is an impossibility. I don't know of any church that is paying $50,000 or more a year to keep a family clothed, fed, housed, and educated. I don't know any church that has made deals with families such that, if they don't abort the children, the church or charities will take care of them or make absolutely sure the child is placed in a loving home. Probably the most that a charity could do would be to give this poor family some food, some clothing, and a cradle. It's simply beyond any church's means.

Pro-life organizations will often advertise their viewpoint with a billboard that shows a beautiful, healthy, white, blue-eyed baby, being held by a happy, white, obviously middle-class mother. But this isn't the problem. The

pro-life stance would be far more convincing if the billboard showed a poor woman with tattered clothes, or holding a Down Syndrome baby or a baby with obvious mental
or physical handicaps. Many of these babies, including babies with AIDS or crack babies, are not easily adoptable,
and they suffer for their whole lives. Is this a true pro-life
stance?

Reframing the Argument

Hillary Clinton, former First Lady, Senator, Secretary of
State, and presidential candidate, tried to change the face
of the argument. In 2005, she reached across party lines,
believing "people of good faith" can find "common ground
in this debate." She looked for the issues we could all agree
on—"increasing women's access to quality health care and
reducing unwanted pregnancy. . . . We should all be able
to agree that we want every child born in this country and
around the world to be wanted, cherished, and loved. The
best way to get there is do more to educate the public about
reproductive health, about how to prevent unsafe and unwanted pregnancies."[13] She said, "We can all recognize that
abortion in many ways represents a sad, even tragic, choice
to many, many women." Both Bill Clinton and Hillary Clinton have said abortion should be "safe, legal, and rare." In
his article about the speech, Andrew Sullivan says, "Hers is
. . . a broadly pro-life position. Not in an absolutist, logi-
cally impeccable fashion—which would require abolishing
all forms of legal abortion immediately—but in a pragmatic, moral sense. In a free society, the ability of a woman
to control what happens to her own body will always and

should always be weighed in the balance against the right of an unborn child to life itself."

Sullivan says, "Clinton's approach is the right one. Acknowledge up-front the pain of abortion and its moral gravity. Defend its legality only as a terrible compromise necessary for the reduction of abortions in general, for the rights of women to control their own wombs, and for the avoidance of unsafe, amateur abortions. And then move to arenas where liberals need have no qualms: aggressive use of contraception and family planning, expansion and encouragement of adoptions, and a rhetorical embrace of the 'culture of life.'"

In discussing Clinton's speech, Sullivan says, "Clinton did one other thing as well. She paid respect to her opponents. She acknowledged the genuine religious convictions of those who oppose all abortion. She recognized how communities of faith have often been the most successful in persuading young women to refrain from teenage sex. She challenged her pro-choice audience by pointing out 'seven percent of American women who do not use contraception account for fifty-three percent of all unintended pregnancies.' She also cited research estimating that 15,000 abortions per year are by women who have been sexually assaulted—one of the several reasons, she said, that morning-after emergency contraception should be made available over the counter. By focusing on contraception, she appeals to all those who oppose abortion but who do not follow the abstinence-only movement's rigid restriction on the surest way to prevent them."

What was the Republican response to Hillary Clinton's effort to find agreement and reach across party lines? She was rebuffed. Rather than trying to resolve this serious issue, Republicans refused to even discuss it. Many Christian Democrats see this as denial, not effective policymaking to help solve a social problem.

Some Christians are willing to broaden this whole debate about abortion, believing pro-life means, truly, to be pro-life. They look for what they call a Consistent Life Ethic. In 1987, some of these people—Catholics, mainline Protestants, and Evangelicals, as well as interfaith and non-religious members—formed a group originally called the "Seamless Garment," based on John 19:23, which describes Jesus' garment as "seamless, woven in one piece." This group, now called Consistent Life, believes if one is against abortion, and is pro-life, this stance has to be consistent for all life. Most of the group's members are Christian Democrats who see a connection between the Democratic Party's stance of defending the life of the poor and the weak and the logical conclusion they would also defend the life of the unborn child. They see a contradiction between a pro-life statement that defends the life of the unborn, but then allows policies that result in the death of hundreds of thousands through war, capital punishment, starvation, and murder. The Seamless Garment Network calls this a "most egregious example of Republican double-speak." Its members' stance on life brings together other stands that relate to peace, justice, human rights, and reverence for life.

Democrats for Life

The Democratic Party has started to address these issues, realizing that its rejection of pro-life members is not consistent with the party's ideals of inclusion. Not every Democrat is pro-choice. Not every Republican is pro-life. But the Democrats had not been welcoming to those who were not pro-choice—until recently. In 1999, the Democrats for Life of America (DFLA) was founded. They recognize that there are 21 million Democrats who are pro-life, which is about one in three Democrats. They see that pro-life does not just mean being "against abortion," but they have a consistent pro-life ethic, which is also against capital punishment and euthanasia. Although they oppose abortion, they provide support for the pregnant woman. They find the tent of the Democratic Party much more conducive to their beliefs because they see Republican policies around this issue are not supporting women. The Republicans have voted against the Violence Against Women Act, the Lilly Ledbetter Fair Pay Act, and the Affordable Care Act, all of which are designed to support women.

The DFLA has issued a "95-10" initiative, which includes fifteen different policy programs that set out to reduce the number of abortions in American by 95 percent in ten years. These programs include funding to increase public awareness of alternatives; comprehensive sex education that includes a discussion of abstinence but also includes education about contraception and sexually transmitted diseases; abortion counseling and education for college students; and tax credits for adoption and domestic violence prevention. The group's policies are aimed at helping women as well as protecting unborn children.[14]

Democrats for Life was formed as a response to the extreme positions both parties have taken, which have not been effective at reducing abortions.

The pro-life approach of Democrats for Life differs from the Republican viewpoint, which endorses abstinence-only programs. Such programs have been found to be ineffective, because they withhold information about sex education. Democrats for Life criticize the Republican Party platform on abortion, comparing it to "having a bunch of tin cans tied to your back bumper—it sure makes a lot of noise but is not very pretty and certainly doesn't accomplish much."[15]

They further criticize the Republicans' gag rule that denies U.S. family planning aid to foreign health care providers. If someone who is working for our government or in the military overseas wants an abortion, even though one would be legal in the United States, that person is not allowed information about where or how to get one.

Women who are poor need assistance to pay for contraceptive services, and to understand their alternatives. Keeping them ill-informed and misinformed, although it may sound morally right to some, does not stop unwanted pregnancies. In fact, it increases the percentages.

There are no easy answers. To stand clearly on one side or the other demands that we have to ignore some biblical, moral, ethical, and/or spiritual responses to these issues. Where do we look for answers? We return to compassion, above all.

Chapter Five

Homosexuals:
Civil Rights, Same-Sex Marriage

"The Lord said, 'who hath made man's mouth?
Or who maketh the dumb or deaf or the seeing
or the blind? Have not I, the Lord?'"

Exodus 4:11

There are millions of homosexuals in the United States of America. Between 3.5 and 10 percent of the population is estimated to be gay, lesbian, bisexual, or transgender.[1] There is much disagreement on whether homosexuals should be equal. The Republican Platform expresses their commitment to equality of race, religion, creed, and national origin, but not to gender equality. The Supreme Court in June, 2015 declared marriage equality for all, not just for heterosexuals. Republicans consider this ruling immoral and unconstitutional.

Same-sex issues relate to how we define a family, to how we understand the nature of homosexuality, and to

111

how we understand the rights of mothers and fathers and children.

A Christian friend of mine told me a few years ago that children are hard-wired to need a mother and a father, so that traditional nuclear marriage is very important for raising children. Yet many cultures raise their children through a community made up of mothers and fathers, aunts and uncles, grandmothers and grandfathers, and sometimes the entire village.

Many would agree that it would be a good idea for children to be raised with a loving mother and a loving father. Others would say that it is most important to love and care for your children and that this is not dependent on male or female or on sexual orientation. Millions of children are raised in one-parent families, either because the mother isn't married, or because of divorce or death of the spouse. Many are raised by relatives; others by homosexual couples. Research has shown that a nontraditional family is no guarantee of failure. Nor is a traditional family a guarantee of wonderful children. It is a fairy-tale expectation to think that we can find some ideal family dynamic throughout our society. It is impossible to legislate that every child has to have a mother and a father and live in a loving nuclear family.

The definition of family has changed throughout our history. Many people see a family as a bond between or among people. This might be two married people without children (such as my husband and me), or married with children, or unmarried with children, or unmarried but living together, or a group of people living communally.

Similarly, the definition of marriage has changed and

expanded. It used to be taken for granted that marriage meant children, and there was tremendous pressure put upon a couple without children to fulfill their obligation and have babies. If they didn't have children, they were considered "selfish" or "different" and therefore "wrong." Some people believe that their own choices and the validity of their own marriages are called into question if individuals are free to go their own way, to find their own love and bliss, whether through being a family with no children, or a same-sex family, or a commune. These people consider those choices dangerous, thinking that too much difference in our society could bring about chaos and a loss of stability. Although there is plenty of chaos and instability in our society, most of it doesn't seem to come from people living their lives differently from the conventional model.

Like abortion, same-sex marriage is a very divisive issue. Yet, by 2015, 60 percent of Americans supported same-sex marriage. Without laws to codify such equality, same-sex couples couldn't make medical decisions for each other. Even if they had been together for decades, they were not allowed to visit each other in the hospital if one of their parents forbade it. If one was dying, the other would not be allowed to hold the hand of the dying partner, because hospitals didn't consider them "family." Instead of bringing a family together at a time of tragedy, a hospital had the right to keep people apart.

Without legal protection, same-sex couples couldn't inherit from each other. Even if their wills were set up to give everything to the surviving partner, the wills could be broken by a parent. These couples weren't eligible for each other's Social Security benefits, even if they'd lived together for longer than most married couples.

Gay couples didn't have the same rights to health care or shared pension plans that heterosexual couples had. Some school districts didn't give the same opportunity to gay teachers that they gave to straight teachers. They were second-class citizens without the same rights as other Americans. The Supreme Court decision has changed all this.

Much anti-gay feeling has arisen from fear that LGBTs would try to promote their lifestyle or prey upon others. But most homosexuals are not promoting their lifestyle or their sexual practices—nor would it do much good. We don't "catch" homosexuality by being near them, and if we are hard-wired as heterosexuals, any sign they put up that says, "Become a homosexual!" won't be very effective.

Homosexuals don't spend all their time involved in homosexual activities. Their lives are about more than just sex. Besides their sexual practices, which they may, or may not, practice more than heterosexuals, they also take care of children, work, do laundry, watch television, cook, and go to movies, art galleries, and the ballet. When heterosexual people think of homosexuals, they often think only about how much sex gay people are having and how they're doing it, rather than seeing the whole person.

Homosexuality as Identity

It is understandable that many people would have some trouble with the idea of homosexuality. There is deep-seated homophobia within many people. Particularly for heterosexual males, the thought of homosexual relationships is repellent. It seems unnatural to them, and, of course, it is unnatural for most of them. Some of this is based on fear—will a homosexual make a pass at them? Will they be raped by a gay man? This fear leads some people to want to forbid any activities they dislike, don't understand, or wouldn't do themselves.

I notice this fear far more in men than in women. I have talked to many heterosexual men who may be tolerant, and who may even be friends with homosexual men, but are emotionally repulsed by the thought of what gay men do. There is something deep-seated about this response, which goes far beyond any belief that comes from an interpretation of Scripture. Some might say this is a natural revulsion to what is offensive to God, but I don't think so. It seems to simply be homophobia, and the reaction I hear from men is much the same as the reaction of some children who learn about sex for the first time. It's the "icky" factor, which contains both disgust and fear, and sometimes fascination.

I don't see this revulsion among women, even women who might believe that homosexuality is morally wrong. When I've talked to heterosexual women about lesbians, they often say, "Well, it's their business" or "I really don't care what women do in the bedroom" or "I guess they're just more attracted to women than men." Some women add, "Considering some of the men I've met, I can understand!" Even those who don't agree with the behavior seem to take it in stride. Some heterosexual men also are not at all repulsed by lesbian sex. In fact, they find it fascinating, and some find it even "chic" to think of women together.

Forbidding homosexuality is not a viable choice. It would mean denying equality to millions of Americans who live in this democracy and, hoping for equal rights, have a sexual orientation or a lifestyle that millions of other Americans don't understand.

Although some Christian groups have programs that try to convert homosexuals to a heterosexual lifestyle, there is no proof this works for most people. Those who are bisexual may have a better chance of making choices, but others are not capable of changing. It's simply who they are, genetically speaking. One of my lesbian friends said, "Since our society promotes heterosexuality and vilifies homosexuality, if someone could have made us straight, we would be straight. We didn't choose to be homosexuals in a society that doesn't accept us."

Some years ago, I asked a gay friend to explain whether he had ever been attracted to a woman. He told me he believed that our sexual responses are on a continuum. There are some people who are on one end, such as he was. He said he is a "totally gay man." He had never been attracted to women, although he could be friends with them. Other people seem to be totally heterosexual (think James Bond!), always attracted to someone from the opposite sex, and never attracted to someone of the same sex. For neither of these groups is there any choice.

Others fall somewhere in between. They might be people who had homosexual feelings at times, perhaps during puberty, but chose not to pursue them and were happy heterosexuals as adults. Others married, and realized they were deeply unhappy because they were gay and had not been willing or able to admit it. They were tired of living a lie, and found that only by choosing who they truly were could they be authentic people. Others were bisexual and found they could choose. At different times in their lives, they pursued relationships with the opposite sex. At other times, they chose someone from the same gender. For some, their time pursuing homosexual relationships filled them with a deep sense of guilt and estrangement. For others, it brought a sense of freedom and even stability. For some bisexuals, the choice of partners depended on their sexual attraction. They found the spirit and personality of the person more compelling than the gender.

For many homosexuals, denying their attraction means denying their integrity and authenticity as human beings. Pretending to be someone they are not seems to them to be a spiritual offense. Some of them have told me that after much struggle, they came to believe that God made them that way. Just as some people are born blind or deaf, they were born as homosexuals.

We don't know why some people are homosexuals. The Lord says that we are not to question why we are made a certain way. In Exodus 4:11, the Lord said, "Who makes a person dumb or deaf, gives sight or makes blind? Is it not I, Yahweh?" In Isaiah, the Lord says, "Does the clay say to its potter, 'What are you doing? Your work has no hands!' . . . It is I who made the earth and I created human beings on it."[2] Romans says, "Something that was made, can it say to its maker: why did you make me this shape? A potter surely has the right over his clay to make out of the same lump either a pot for special use or one for ordinary use."[3]

Why are some people created as gay and others as straight? Why do some report they have no attraction to the opposite sex and never have? Why do some say they knew, from an early age, that they were different, and wondered why God had created them that way? Is it possible God made them this way for a reason? Or are they the rejects? If they're rejects, why is God making junk?

There are heterosexuals who accept homosexuals provided they're not practicing homosexuals. In this view, as many as ten percent of the population should never allow themselves to be intimate, never love and commit to one other person, never experience the joys of sexuality, never accept their true identity, and never find the fulfillment others find with another human, just because they were born "different." Our government policy toward a large percentage of our population depends on how we view homosexuality. Our view often depends on our interpretation of Scripture, our understanding of spirituality, and our experience of relating to homosexuals.

The Scriptural Basis Against Homosexuality

Many Christians are unclear what to think about this difficult subject. Others say the Bible is very clear. There are Scriptural verses that seem to be against homosexuality, and there are some that seem to take no stand. There are still others that seem to support loving bonds, even between two people of the same sex.

What does Jesus have to say about homosexuality? Nothing. What does Jesus have to say about same-sex marriages? Nothing. What does Paul have to say about same-sex marriages? Nothing. There is no mention of homosexuality in the Ten Commandments. No prophet discusses it. It's not found in the Gospels, although it certainly existed in biblical times. There is no mention anywhere in the Bible of committed homosexual relationships. There is no mention of lesbianism.

There are, however, verses referring to homosexual acts between men that can be found in both the Hebrew Scriptures and New Testament.

The lack of verses specifically addressing this topic leads both conservatives and liberals to interpret the biblical stance about homosexual relationships in the light of other verses. More conservative Christians will interpret the stance of Jesus and Paul as being pro-marriage, since they mention the bonds between husband and wife, thereby implying they are for heterosexual marriage and against homosexual unions. To do this, these Christians have to overlook the fact that neither Jesus nor Paul ever married.

During the course of writing this book, I have read innumerable interpretations of both sides of the issue. Personally, I am not convinced by either stance. The conservatives, such as Focus on the Family, have to interpret a number of verses out of context, or else read into the Bible and say that something is "Gospel Truth" when it isn't. Their interpretations don't look at the overall historical context of the time, nor do they involve much deep study about the origins of certain words used in the Bible.

More liberal interpreters are more apt to look at the specific words and how they were used in biblical times, and at the context of the times, but they still can find no proof that the Bible is in favor of homosexuals. They tend to make sweeping generalizations, although they are more apt to admit they are still struggling with the issues. What seems so clear to people of both sides always demands some interpretation.

I don't believe there are clear biblical answers about this issue. I do believe it is worth exploring, however, and that there are some spiritual answers conservative and moderate and liberal Christians can agree on.

What does the Bible say about homosexuality? The texts most often cited (which I will quote in full later) are Genesis 19, Leviticus 18 and 20, Romans 1, I Corinthians 6, and I Timothy 1:10. Out of the entire Bible, there are fewer than ten verses about this subject. Most of these are ambiguous, and some don't even mention homosexuality specifically, but talk in general about degrading sexual practices. Compare these to the dozens, or hundreds, of verses about money, about oppression, about how a king should rule, about incest, about hypocrisy, about quarreling. In fact, if you look up the word "homosexual" in a Concordance, chances are you'll only find one verse—I Corinthians 6:9. Because I was writing *Jesus Rode a Donkey*, I also checked to see how many references there are to donkeys—about 200. There has been an unbalanced amount of discussion about what people think is in the Bible, but isn't.

The Hebrew Scriptures

When Christians try to understand the meaning of certain biblical texts, they take various approaches. I once asked a fundamentalist what she thought about homosexuality and she answered, "I don't know. I have to ask my minister." Fundamentalists usually will turn to the authority of the Bible or the preacher to learn what a proper response should be. They will take the Bible literally, at face value, according to whatever translation they feel is correct. If there are contradictions, they try to square them up in some way, which sometimes works and sometimes doesn't. They generally will not study the context or the derivation of the word or put it into an overall biblical theology.

Others, however, will study the text. They will do this by looking at the original meaning of the word and then looking at the context of the times. Although many think liberals tend to be too contextual in their analysis and conservatives tend to be too literal, every Christian picks and chooses verses to create an interpretation, particularly when the interpretation is ambiguous. None of us are perfect in our interpretation.

Focus on the Family, a national conservative Christian organization, begins its analysis of homosexuality by looking at Genesis 1 and 2, which define us as male and female, created in the image of God. We are asked to be fruitful and multiply. The organization's reasoning says that because we are made as male and female, we are asked to have sexual relations with each other and to have children to propagate the human race. Homosexuals don't procreate; therefore, homosexuals are not fulfilling the natural order and the command of creation.[4]

Genesis 1 and 2 say nothing about other types of relationships that don't procreate but are recognized in the Bible—married without children, friendships, being single, being celibate—but yet we don't condemn these. The Church recognizes all these relationships, and does not deny the loving bonds many of us have with our spouses, whether we have children or not. If we take this argument to its logical conclusion, we can see that neither Jesus nor Paul was following God's commandment.

Most churches recognize that marriage is not just for procreation. The Catholic Church marries those who are infertile, and those who are past childbearing age. The Anglican Church, at the Ninth Lambeth Conference in 1958, passed a resolution that says "sexual intercourse is not by any means the only language of earthly love . . . it is a giving and receiving in the unity of two free spirits which is in itself good. . . . Therefore it is utterly wrong to say that . . . such intercourse ought not be engaged in except with the willing intention of children."[5]

The first reference to homosexuality occurs in the story of Lot found in Genesis 19. When angels came to Lot's town of Sodom, Lot welcomed them to his home. The men of the town gathered outside his home and asked him to give them the angels (it is presumed the angels were male) so they could "know" them, which is usually interpreted as having sexual relations with them. Lot didn't want to be inhospitable by throwing out the angels, so he offered his two daughters as a consolation prize. The Bible says nothing about whether his behavior toward his daughters was right or wrong, or about the obvious bisexual choices of the townsmen. But the angels intervened, telling Lot that God was going to destroy Sodom and that he should take his family and escape. Lot and his daughters made it to a cave in the mountains, although the daughters' fiancés refused to leave. The daughters then made their father drunk, had sex with him, and got pregnant, presumably in order to preserve the family line. It is a strange justification for incest, but it's one more example of all the bad sex surrounding the story of Lot and his family.

If we look more closely at this passage, Lot doesn't mention their sexual behavior, but instead tells the men not to insult his guests. These men were seeking to violate the sanctuary of his roof.[6] Gray Temple writes that "Traditional Jewish interpretations of that chapter grasped the principle better than we do: the Sodomites were first and foremost inhospitable; they thought it good sport to humiliate foreign guests."[7]

Ezekiel 16:49-50 says that God destroyed Sodom (and Gomorrah) for their sins of arrogance, decadence, and complacency: "Behold, this was the iniquity of the sister Sodom, pride, fullness of bread, and abundance of idleness was in her and in her daughters, neither did she strengthen the hand of the poor and needy." The Book of Ecclesiasticus and the Book of Wisdom (both found in the Catholic Bible but not in the Protestant Bible) also mention pride as the sin of Sodom, because the Sodomites did not help the poor and the needy. Jesus implied that the sin of Sodom was inhospitality, which was why it was destroyed.[8]

The sins of Sodom were many. The story in Genesis 19 is not about any kind of normal sexual behavior; it is about gang rape. Whether performed by homosexuals or heterosexuals, this does not establish any kind of normative sexuality. Just as we wouldn't turn to these stories to tell us about heterosexual love, we have no reason to turn to them to understand homosexual love. Since other books of the Bible interpret this story and never mention homosexuality, the story seems to be about violent sexual behavior, incest, inhospitality, and degradation. We can't use these verses to condemn homosexuality. They simply are not about that.

The strongest language about homosexuality comes from Leviticus 18 and 20, which are part of the section of Leviticus called the Holiness Code or Holiness Laws. The verses usually cited are from Leviticus 18:22, which says, "You shall not lie with a male as with a woman: it is an abomination," and from Leviticus 20, which says, "If a man lies with a male as with a woman, both of them have committed an abomination. They shall be put to death; their blood is upon them."

This seems to be very clear—homosexuality is wrong! In fact, it seems to say this is so wrong that some believe homosexuals should be executed. Kevin Swanson, the head of a Religious Liberties conference, believes this and preaches strongly with great conviction and flailing of arms. He invited Ted Cruz, Mike Huckabee, and Rick Santorum to speak at his conference. They did and thereby endorsed his views and made their anti-gay attitudes clear.

If we look at other laws within this section of Leviticus, we can see that people who commit other abominations also are to be put to death: children who curse their parents,[9] people who worship idols,[10] adulterers,[11] and those who practice bestiality.[12]

In addition to these laws, there are a number of other laws in Leviticus forbidding certain practices, such as the inbreeding of cattle, sowing fields with two kinds of seed, wearing garments made of two different materials, and harvesting fruit trees which are less than five years old. Round haircuts and tattoos are forbidden. Having sexual relations during a woman's menstrual cycle is forbidden.

One can take these verses at face value. Even then, we pick and choose which verses we'll follow. Few of us believe that adulterers should be put to death, partly because that would mean a number of self-proclaimed Christians would now be dead. (Newt Gingrich, Donald Trump, Bill Clinton, Ted Haggard, Governor Mark Sanford, and John McCain, for starters.) Few Christians would suggest we kill our children if they curse us (although some might want to!), and most of us wear garments made of different fabrics.

So if we don't follow the letter of the law of most of these codes, how can we interpret them? Theologians look carefully at the historical context and the specific words to understand why these laws were written and why these practices were an abomination to God.

The Ancient Holiness Codes

The Holiness Codes were established when the Israelites entered the land of Canaan, where Canaanites worshipped the god Molech. The Israelites were establishing a new nation within a country where other laws and practices prevailed. Peter Gomes, former Plummer Professor of Christian Morals at Harvard College and a gay Republican, analyzes these passages. He says these rules were designed for "nation building; their setting is the entry into a promised but very foreign land. These are fundamental laws for the formation of a frontier community."[13] These laws were used for "cultural identity, protection, and procreation."[14] Any behavior that did not lead to populating the country was outlawed. Homosexual behavior did not lead to procreation. In a frontier community, it was imperative to produce children to create a new nation.

Dr. Gary Rendsburg, who holds the Endowed Chair in Jewish History at Rutgers University and is an expert in the Bible and ancient Semitic languages, says, "There is no doubt in my mind that homosexuality is totally forbidden in these passages. However, these passages reflect the mores of 3,000 years ago. I do keep some of these laws. I still observe the Sabbath, I still keep kosher, but I don't stone my children if they curse me, and I don't own slaves. What always strikes me as a Jew looking at Christian opposition to homosexuality, [is] if Christians were so interested in upholding the laws of the Torah, why aren't Christians observing the dietary laws, and Sabbath on the seventh day? [There are] all sorts of ritual laws Christians won't observe, so why are they so concerned about this one? I don't think we should stone someone for collecting wood on the Sabbath. I don't believe that men should inherit and not women, unless there are no men in the family."[15]

We don't follow most of the other Holiness Codes set forth in Leviticus that tell us how to act. Although these Codes include prohibitions that we still follow—against rape, incest, adultery, necrophilia, and bestiality—they also prohibit celibacy, nudity, and birth control. Men trim their beards, even though Leviticus tells them not to. Women wear male clothing, such as jeans and slacks, even though they're told not to. We ignore certain passages, deciding they no longer apply, and follow others. In ignoring certain passages, we don't dig deeper into why there are certain prohibitions. What was the context of the day that relates to mixing fibers? What kind of sexuality was prohibited, and why?

Sexuality as Power

To better understand these passages, some scholars look at how sexual relationships functioned in earlier societies. Until 1869, the idea of homosexuality and heterosexuality did not exist as we think of it today. Sexuality was defined as power relationships, and what was clearly "wrong" was for someone to be used or manipulated by a stronger person.

Many sources emphasized that sex was about power and the natural hierarchy. For men to engage in homosexual practices meant one of the two men had to be in the weak, passive position. This was not "manly" and was an affront to male identity.

Sometimes the passive partner was a young boy, who was often abused by an older man for his own sexual pleasure. This was a fairly common practice in Greece, Rome, and Canaan. The Israelites had laws against it for several reasons. First of all, there was an imbalance of power and lack of mutuality in these relationships. Second, the Jews were new to the land of Canaan. They were forming a cultural identity that was different from, and even in opposition to, the identity of Canaanites. Since homosexuality was a more common practice in Canaan, the Jews differentiated themselves from the Canaanites' sexual practices, as well as from their practices of idolatry, their dietary laws, and so on.

Other scholars look at how sexual identity is defined. "The human race used to divide itself into gender identities of 'strong' and 'weak,' not 'queer' and 'straight.' In the ancient cultures of Greece, Rome, Egypt, Sumer, Babylon, and throughout the eastern Mediterranean, there were no words for homosexuality, homosexual, heterosexuality, or heterosexual. They had specific words for specific acts, but not general words for general concepts. The crime was not homosexuality. It was always something else."[16]

Positive Verses About Same-Sex Orientation

Notice, in the Hebrew Scriptures, that nothing is said about lesbians. If one believes these verses are adamantly against homosexuals, it might be thought that lesbians are not mentioned because none existed during that time. But there clearly were lesbians. They can be found in the erotic poetry of Sappho of the island of Lesbos as well as in various paintings. Some interpret these verses and believe lesbianism is implied by the prohibitions against male sexual behavior. But there is absolutely nothing in any of these verses suggesting this.

Those who believe that the Bible does not condemn same-sex relationships look to the story of David and Jonathan from I Samuel 18–20 and II Samuel 1. The Bible says Jonathan "loved him [David] like his very self."[17] "They made a covenant with each other."[18] "And Jonathan stripped himself of the robe that was upon him, and gave it to David, and his garments, even to his sword, and to his bow, and to his girdle."[19] It sounds as if he got down to his undies, or less, and to the modern mind, this seems a bit suspect. And it goes on with further details. David and Jonathan took great delight in each other and kissed each other.[20] David said to Jonathan, "Greatly beloved were you to me; your love to me was wonderful, passing the love of women."[21]

Any discussion and interpretation of these passages

leads to huge debates and great fervor on both sides. I was told by one scholar I consulted to leave this passage alone, because it will just bring about fire and brimstone. But if we are to struggle with other Hebrew Scripture passages related to this subject, we definitely have to struggle with this one.

Focus on the Family sees this as a strong friendship, and says that revisionists try to interpret it as having a sexual component and that this is "morally wrong." However, there is nothing to revise here. There is only interpretation. What are we to make of one man recognizing that his love for another man surpasses his love for women? We don't know what this means in its biblical context. We do know this is what a homosexual says to another homosexual. But in the case of David and Jonathan, it's impossible to know what is meant. None of us have peered into the tent to see what David and Jonathan were doing to express their love for each other. We haven't followed them up to the hillside to see what they were doing. We can interpret, but it's impossible to know which interpretation is accurate.

We do know they kissed each other. Kisses are exchanged in friendship, and they are exchanged in sexual relationships. Nothing is said about what kind of kiss this was. We do know that the Bible makes no condemnation of the covenant they made between them, the kisses they exchanged, or the fact that they loved each other more than they loved someone of the opposite sex.

We do know that both Jonathan and David were married to women, and David had other sexual relationships with women besides with his seven wives. But we also know that his love for Jonathan surpassed these other relationships.

However we interpret these passages—as being about homosexual love, or about friendship that is greater than heterosexual love—we know that the Bible does not condemn this same-sex relationship. The Bible recognizes the strength of this loving bond between two people of the same gender.

The New Testament

What about the New Testament passages? As Christians, some would say we need to take them even more seriously. As with the Hebrew Scriptures, there are only a few passages mentioning homosexual acts.

I Timothy has a list of sins: "Those who kill their father or mother, or murderers, fornicators, sodomites, slave traders, liars, perjurers, whatever else is contrary to the sound teaching that conforms to the glorious Gospel."[22]

Notice, nothing specifically here is said about homosexuals, and certainly nothing here is said about lesbians, although the word "sodomites" is thought to be referring to homosexuals (not recognizing that some heterosexuals also commit sodomy and lesbians are unable to naturally commit sodomy). However, the Greek word for "sodomites" does not clearly refer to homosexuals. It's a rare term, and is thought to refer to a man who uses male prostitutes or a man who has sex with boys.[23]

The word in the original text for "male prostitutes" means "soft." As Catherine Griffith writes in an article on the Bible and same-sex relationships: "Biblical scholars say that the word in ancient texts referred to luxurious clothing, rich and delicate food, a gentle breeze, or was used to condemn immorality and faults associated with effeminacy, such as being weak, lazy, lustful, decadent, or cowardly. It had no relation to the gender of a man's preferred sexual partner, but more to a kind of soft decadence."[24]

In I Corinthians 6, Paul has a similar list: fornicators, idolaters, adulterers, male prostitutes (although nothing is said about female prostitutes), sodomites, thieves, the greedy, drunkards, revilers, robbers. In the King James version, the list includes "the effeminate, and abusers of themselves with mankind, and extortioners." For male prostitutes, Paul uses the word *malakoi* (from the original Greek) or *arsenokoitai*, which is translated as "sodomites." *Malakoi* means "soft, overripe, or squishy." It may not even refer to male sexual behavior at all, but to one who was "soft" on self-control.[25] The term *arsenokoitai* is only used twice in the New Testament and never in the Hebrew Scriptures, although the translation uses the same word as is used in Leviticus—sodomites. There is no clear translation of this word, although it was used later by Hippolytus to refer to a man who sleeps with boys. Author Robin Scroggs, in *The New Testament and Homosexuality*, suggests it might refer to "a young man who inveigles himself into the erotic affections of an elderly man in order to get included in his will and abscond with his estate."[26]

In Romans 1:18–32, Paul talks about sexual degradations and unnatural acts, saying, "Their women exchanged natural intercourse (*chresis*) for unnatural (*para physin*) . . . and in the same way also the men, giving up natural (*physiken*) intercourse (*chresis*) with women, were consumed (*exekauthesan*) with passion (*orexis*) for one another. Men committed shameless acts with men and received in their own persons the due penalty for their error."[27]

In this chapter, Paul uses the word *chresis*, which is sometimes translated as "intercourse," though it actually is a term meaning "usage" that "referred primarily to food and sex."[28] It was not a term that implied relationship or mutuality; it was about exploiting another for one's own purposes. Paul, as do many of us, opposes one person using another.

Notice, also, that there is nothing said about sexual behavior between two females. Looking carefully at this passage, one can understand how it got misinterpreted, because we presume that women's "unnatural" acts means unnatural acts with each other. But a more careful reading of this passage shows that nothing is said about women with women; it only mentions women exchanging natural relations for those that are unnatural.

The focus is on the word "unnatural." According to Paul, "nature" has more to do with what is expected or accepted rather than that which is morally wrong. What were women's unnatural acts? For a woman to be aggressive in sex was unnatural. For a woman to be flirtatious, or to mount the man, was unnatural.[29]

Homosexuality was not as natural among Jews as it was among Greeks and Romans. What was wrong, according to the Jewish code, was the domination of one sexual partner by another, in many cases men exploiting boys, or men put in a weaker position. The Jews objected to pedophilia, but the objects were never girls; they were upper-class boys subjected to the humiliation of someone in power using them.[30]

Sexuality was also unnatural if men were swept away by passion and lost their rationality. Their lust showed their weakness. Moderation was the best standard.

The word for "unnatural" is used in this section to discuss other issues that are not "natural," but not morally wrong. It's the same word used by Paul in 11:24 to clarify God's unnatural action when he "engrafted Gentiles onto the Jewish olive tree." I Corinthians 11:2–16 says long hair for women and short hair for men are natural, so if a woman has short hair (as I do), it is unnatural but (I hope) not morally wrong.

Unnatural sex might be unequal sex, since the cultural norm of the Christian era meant one partner was active and one passive, so anything but the missionary position would be considered unnatural.

The more important thing about this chapter from Romans is the way Paul phrases his argument. He focuses on many ways we dishonor God—through passions out of control, by "injustice, rottenness, greed and malice . . . envy, murder, wrangling, treachery and spite," libeling, slandering, rudeness, arrogance, boastfulness; by being "enterprising in evil, rebellious to parents, without brains, honor, love, or pity." According to Paul, people guilty of any of these things deserve to die. Considering how many different sins are given, that means us too—and all the presidential candidates! We only have to apply these ways of dishonoring God to the candidates to see how many of them deserve to die in Paul's analysis. Yet how many of us are without any of these sins?

Just as Paul makes sure we're all included in his long list of sins, he adds one more—judgment. "It is yourself that you condemn when you judge others, since you behave in the same way as those you are condemning. . . . do you think you will escape God's condemnation?"[31]

Paul makes two important points with this argument. First, he lets readers know they should not judge, because they commit the same sins. He's not concerned about prohibiting lustful homosexuality, which is just a symptom of a larger problem. Instead, he prohibits judgment. This same idea is repeated in many Bible verses—"Judge not," "Do not judge that you be not judged," "There is only one Lawgiver and one judge." "Let he who is without sin cast the first stone."[32] The "same way" refers not to homosexuality, but rather to ingratitude to God and intemperate passions such as greed and lust.

Paul then finishes the letter to the Romans by admonishing his readers not to pass judgment on others, "but resolve instead never to put a stumbling block or hindrance in the way of another. I know and am persuaded through the Lord Jesus that nothing is unclean in itself; but it is unclean for anyone who thinks it unclean." These verses from Romans are not a description of a healthy sexual relationship, but of sex that uses another person.

Paul saw the problem of homosexuality as being about lust, avarice, passions out of control. Most of us would agree. When we read about the bathhouses of San Francisco that were a breeding ground for the AIDS epidemic, we can recognize that this leads to great harm to individuals and society. When we read about, or take part in, any sexual behavior that uses or abuses another person, we understand what this form of degradation can do to the human spirit.

If we look carefully at all of these passages, we notice that out of ten references, most are not about homosexuality. Some that are used by various groups to show the anti-homosexuality of the Bible are actually about marriage, such as Genesis 1 and 2. Most of the other ones are in a list of degrading sexual behaviors, such as gang rape, that would be condemned whether they were done by heterosexuals or homosexuals. Probably most of us can agree there are degrading and abusive sexual acts—rape, incest, pedophilia, and sex trafficking, where women are sold into prostitution. Yet we don't condemn heterosexuality because some heterosexual practices may be degrading.

Other passages, such as the one in Romans, are actually an argument that ends up condemning the act of being judgmental. It seems that Leviticus 18 and 20 are the only two passages that seem fairly blatant in their condemnation, and even these verses need to be read in the context of the time. They do not state clearly whether all homosexual behavior is condemned, or only that which is degrading. To interpret these passages as condemning all homosexual behavior means we have to decide that these passages say something not clearly stated.

Notice also that none of these passages are about homosexual identity. The idea of homosexual identity was foreign to those in both the Hebrew Scriptures and the New Testament. Almost all of these verses refer to the "debauched pagan expression" of homosexuality.[33] If you know homosexuals in long-term loving relationships, you know from your experience that these lists of immoral behaviors are not referring to them. The Rt. Rev. Gray Temple says in *Gay Unions*, "Those who insist that our gay sisters and brothers in the church are . . . impure or debased, or that they are uniquely prone to the actual sins that Paul just described, have simply not bothered to get to know their fellow Christians."[34]

A Consistent Christian Response to Homosexuality

Regardless of the interpretation of these various passages, there is one consistent response that comes from the churches—to love and respect the Other. We see this in the way Jesus related to women, to prostitutes, to tax collectors, to those who were different and on the fringes of society. For most churches, hate crimes are not acceptable Christian behavior. Humiliation and rejection are not acceptable responses to homosexuals.

Churches take various stances on homosexuality. The United Church of Christ, Methodist, the Metropolitan Church, the Episcopal Church, the Evangelical Lutheran Church, and the Presbyterian Church USA (PCUSA) ordain gays. The Episcopal Church, amidst great controversy, ordained an openly gay bishop and has now ordained a lesbian bishop.

Some churches perform gay marriages. The Metropolitan Community Churches have an explicit ministry to gays. The United Church of Christ and the Society of Friends decide, on an individual basis within each church, whether they will perform gay marriages.

Most, and perhaps all, Christian churches ordain gay men and women, as long as the church does not know that they're gay. Notice the Catholic scandal about child abuse by priests. It almost always involves boys rather than girls.

We are naive if we think churches do not have gay ministers and priests. From my own limited experience, I have known at least three women married to Protestant ministers who later learned their husbands were gay. The men hoped a marriage would, somehow, "cure" them, and then realized they were not living an authentic life and could no longer hide their sexual orientation. Divorce, and usually leaving the church, followed soon after.

From my years attending an interdenominational seminary, I knew several gay priests, some of them practicing homosexuals. My friends at a Catholic seminary told me this was not unusual. In fact, it is estimated that 10 to 50 percent of Catholic priests are gay, some of them practicing homosexuals, which goes against their vows of chastity. Obviously some of them are pedophiles, using and abusing young boys. The Catholic Church is now trying to remove gays from the priesthood, which means that gay priests have several alternatives—all of which raise ethical considerations. They can deny their homosexuality, thereby denying who they are; they can leave the priesthood, thereby denying their understanding of their calling to serve God through this ministry; or they can "out" each other, thereby betraying each other. The Catholic Church, which already lacks enough priests to serve all their parishes, will have to decide what to do when 10 to 50 percent of its priests, many of them kind, compassionate, and loving people who minister well to others, suddenly are no longer there.

Pope Francis has taken a very compassionate tone toward homosexuals. "If a homosexual person is of good will and is in search of God, I am no one to judge." He has not overturned the Catholic stand that says homosexual acts are a sin, but he has changed the tone of condemnation that came from the Catholic Church as it still often comes from Protestant churches, although even Protestant churches are aware that they have members who are gay and have wanted to become more welcoming. And, of course, both the Republican and Democratic parties know that there are millions of voters who are LGBT and, although most of them vote Democrat, some do vote Republican and it's not a good idea to alienate them.

If we try to make social policy based on a few verses, which are interpreted differently depending on the view of the Christian reading them, the research, the knowledge of the original Hebrew, and the knowledge of the historical context, we may, in the process, be doing great harm to millions of Americans. Some Christians say they truly love the homosexuals but don't approve of them. I have not yet figured out how to love people while condemning their lifestyle, judging their relationships, and being able to accept them only if they become different and, in the process, compromise their authenticity. There are many Christians who say they love the sinner but not the sin, yet gays often attest to the fact that they don't feel loved, only condemned, regardless of whether the judgment comes with a hug or not.

A Spiritual Approach to Homosexuality

Sometimes, when biblical verses are not clear, a Christian might turn to other forms of spirituality rather than to Bible verses to look for answers.

Many Christians believe in ongoing revelation. They believe that the Holy Spirit continues to lead us. Discerning the work of the Spirit is, of course, not a sure-fire thing, but then interpreting a Bible passage is not a sure-fire thing either.

If a Christian slave owner were trying to discern a Christian response to slavery, he might begin by looking at the Bible and noticing that it seems to condone slavery. Owning another person seems to be part of an accepted social structure in both the Hebrew Scriptures and New Testament. He might reflect on the meaning of that kind of control over another. He might pray about it. He might realize that it doesn't "feel" right. He might talk to slaves, or other slave owners. He might notice mistreatment of slaves by other slave owners and recognize this as immoral and uncaring. He might first decide that owning slaves is fine for him because he treats them well, but then decide his stance toward owning slaves is wrong. He frees them and, in retrospect, believes he made the right decision.

A spiritual approach to homosexuality might take the same course. People might begin by studying the Bible verses. They might talk to a variety of homosexuals, asking questions, visiting a church where there are openly gay men and women, talking to ministers and priests. They might observe gay relationships. Or they might follow the example of Jesus, who dined with prostitutes and tax collectors and people considered "sinners," and let the Holy Spirit lead them to discern what they are to think and believe and feel about this situation. Of course, the dinner party won't be a success if one half of the table is judging the other half.

Christians might reflect on what it means to be an authentic human being, without denying flaws, but also without denying how one has been created. They might try to figure out how to treat someone who is "born that way."

They might then think about how they, who are in loving, intimate relationships, can ever deny intimacy to others. They might think about how they wouldn't deny loving partnerships to those who are blind, deaf, or disabled. Can they, in all good conscience, legislate that others are not allowed to ever have the joys of closeness and partnership? They might meditate on the injustices the gay person encounters, sometimes daily, and on how they would feel if those same injustices happened to them.

They might, purposefully, seek out homosexuals and begin asking questions, to better understand their situation, and to better understand that these people are neighbors who cannot be ignored. Believing the Constitution and Bible are for everyone, they might look at how their attitudes or behavior or stances deny equal rights to others. They might recognize that the Constitution gives equal rights to everyone and, if they don't like homosexuals, they have the right not to associate closely with them, while also recognizing their own moral stances should not determine national policy.

Most of my gay friends are in long-term relationships; some of them are married, either through a church or through a ceremony of commitment. I never sought them out. I didn't have to, since my normal course of living brought me in contact with a number of gays and lesbians. Our paths crossed, and in a number of cases friendships developed, perhaps because there was no judgment either way. I attended the marriage of one such friend, and talked to another before, and after, he got married. The profound joy and love that I witness makes it impossible for me to condemn them, because my judgment would go against everything I've learned about spirituality. There is simply too much care and beauty around their relationships. I find the authenticity, wisdom, compassion, and kindness of several of these friends so profound that my spiritual life has been immeasurably enriched by knowing them.

A Democratic Party Approach to Homosexuality

The Bible is silent about homosexuality as identity and about committed homosexual relationships. We can't form national policy based on our own religious interpretations of the Bible. If a democracy is to protect its citizens, what rights do homosexuals have, and what does the Constitution say about equal rights?

The Declaration of Independence and the Constitution specifically state that we will not form national policy or behavior based on our own religion's interpretations of the Bible. There is a consistent movement, through two centuries of amendments to the Constitution, toward equality for all of our citizens. First the Constitution granted equality to propertied males; then to black men; then to women.

What Might Our Response Be?

Every objection I've heard to homosexuals having equal rights seems to come from fear, including a fear of inappropriate behavior that would also be considered inappropriate for heterosexuals. Because there is no evidence that anyone can "make" someone become a homosexual, and because what my neighbors do in their bedroom is of little concern to me, whether they're homosexual or heterosexual, the focus on this issue seems to be masking something else. Families and marriages are not at risk because there is a gay person in the neighborhood. Evidence shows that the presence of a gay person or relationship has no effect on someone else's relationship, in the same way that my neighbors' divorce has no effect on my marriage.

Although Republicans talk about "defense of marriage" and making sure only heterosexuals can marry, marriage is not in any danger from the gays. There has never been any government policy that has said they want to stop traditional marriage and only allow gay people to get married.

Many Christians agree, believing that wherever love and commitment reside, the union should be blessed. Some churches recognize the spirituality of this commitment and have marriage ceremonies for same-sex couples. Although tradition has defined marriage as being between a man and a woman, some Christians recognize another viewpoint on marriage. The Rt. Rev. Gray Temple, an Episcopalian priest and author of *Gay Unions: In the Light of Scripture, Tradition, and Reason,* defines marriage as "a relationship between two persons consisting of human courage intersecting divine grace."[35]

C. S. Lewis, in his classic book *Mere Christianity*, says, "The Christian conception of marriage is one: the other is the quite different question—how far Christians, if they are voters . . . ought to try to force their views of marriage on the rest of the community by embodying them in [their] laws. A great many people seem to think that if you are a

Christian yourself you should try to make [it] difficult for everyone. I do not think that. At least I know I should be very angry if the Mohammedans tried to prevent the rest of us from drinking wine. My own view is that the Churches should frankly recognize that the majority of . . . people are not Christians and, therefore, cannot be expected to live Christian lives. There ought to be two distinct kinds of marriage: one governed by the State with rules enforced on all citizens, the other governed by the Church with rules enforced by her on her own members."[36]

His words raise important questions: Do democracy and equality demand that we recognize the rights of everyone? Or should our own personal morality influence decisions made for everyone else? With any new law, we should ask who does this law harm? And who does this law benefit? Forbidding equal rights to anyone because of sexual orientation is as undemocratic as forbidding rights to anyone because of race or gender or age. Of course, these things are done, but they are not just. Any law that forbids equal rights harms those who want to be part of our democratic society.

Some Christians say same-sex marriage harms society. I know, from my own experience, that the gay marriage of a neighbor or friend has no negative effect on my own marriage, nor do I see it as having any negative effect on others.

What are the consequences to society when we carry an attitude of hate or a desire to forbid the rights of others? How do our political and religious decisions change when we ask homosexuals about their lives, about their concerns, about their spirituality? Where does the Holy Spirit lead us on this issue of such concern to so many?

Chapter Six

War and Peace

*"Blessed are the peacemakers; they shall
be recognized as children of God."*

Matthew 5:9

How seriously are we to take these words of Jesus?
How seriously do we take the image of Jesus as the Prince of
Peace? We talk about peace, we talk about "thou shalt not
kill," but many Christians believe that this commandment
is about murdering rather than killing in general, and that
it's applicable to individuals, but not to society.

For 2,000 years, Christians have struggled with this question: To what extent can a Christian commit violence and
take part in war? Their answers take a number of forms, all
of which are recognized, at least through lip service, by the
U.S. government.

For some Christians, the answer is an absolute. Under no
circumstances should a Christian take part in any war. They
look at the example of the life of the Prince of Peace: his
refusal to become a militant Messiah in order to overcome

the oppressive rule of the Romans, the many words of Paul and Jesus to leave all strife aside, to love the neighbor—even when the neighbor is an enemy. Although the Hebrew Scriptures are filled with stories of wars, mayhem, murder, brutality, and the desire to have God smite the enemy, these attitudes are not found in the New Testament. There are no verses about war in the New Testament, except in the Book of Revelation, which deals with God's war, not ours.

This was the stance of all Christians beginning with Jesus and lasting at least 150 years. From approximately AD 150 until around AD 300 there were very few Christians in the military. Most refused military service. Some were executed for their stance, and they were considered martyrs for their faith.[1] In 314 the Church, under Emperor Constantine, opened the military service to Christians. In 325 Constantine presided over the Council of Nicea, and Christianity became the state religion.

In his book *God or Nations*, Dr. William Durland says, "Numerous disciplines of the church taught categorically that one could not be a soldier and a Christian at the same time. A church order from Egypt reads, 'they shall not receive into the church one of the emperor's soldiers. If they have received him he shall refuse to kill if commanded to do so. If he does not refrain he shall be rejected.'"[2]

The Peace Churches—which include the Church of the Brethren, the Mennonites, the Quakers, and the United Church of Christ—believe war is not justified, and Christians from these denominations generally do not take part in war. Why? The Mennonite Church USA says, "We believe that peace is the will of God. God created the world in peace, and God's peace is most fully revealed in Jesus

Christ, who is our peace and the peace of the whole world. Led by the Holy Spirit, we follow Christ in the way of peace doing justice, bringing reconciliation, and practicing non-resistance, even in the face of violence and warfare. . . . This is our hope: The biblical vision of a day when nations will no longer learn war,[3] a day when God will wipe away all tears and when death, mourning, crying and pain will be no more."[4]

The Church of the Brethren focuses on the costs of war, recognizing that millions of children are killed, wounded, or displaced by war, and that the US government spends one hundred times more on its military than it does on aiding the world's poor. Since the beginning of their Church, Brethren have turned away from violence as a means of solving interpersonal or international problems. The basis for this conviction is firmly rooted in the New Testament, and more specifically in Jesus' teaching on loving our enemies and Paul's admonition that Christians seek to live peaceably with all and that they strive to overcome evil with good.

Quakers ask us all, when confronted with war and terrorism, to formulate "a carefully considered response that honors and affirms that of God in all humankind." They ask us to sow "the seeds of compassion and forgiveness even for those we may consider our fiercest enemies." And they ask for "effective engagement in and promotion of international forums that provide a voice for groups that are oppressed."[5]

Christians have not had a good history of working toward peace. We demonize the other side, so we can more easily kill the enemy. We willingly go along with what our nation asks of us, whether or not the war is justified. Like the enemies we abhor, we too have killed civilians with our guns and bombs. We may speak of peace, but we do not have a history of being peacemakers. We justify war because we feel we have no choice, but we have done little to create a world in which war is not necessary.

The Conscientious Objector

There are a number of Christians (and other spiritual people) who refuse to go to war. The United States government recognizes this stand and allows Christians, as well as others, to take a stand against war for religious reasons or for reasons of conscience. When the Constitution was being drafted, the Founding Fathers considered adding a clause to recognize the status of the Conscientious Objector. The clause never became part of the Constitution. However, CO status became legal in World War I, for those who could identify themselves as members of one of the historic peace churches—the Amish, Jehovah's Witnesses, Mennonite, Church of the Brethren, and Quaker. After World War II any Christian, on a matter of conscience, could apply for CO status. During the Vietnam War, the requirement for CO status was broadened to include anyone's philosophical, moral, or religious beliefs. Conscientious objector status is not selective—a CO has to be against all wars, not just against a specific war. An applicant cannot pick and choose which wars to fight.[6]

Some believe if you love your neighbor you can't kill because everyone is your neighbor. They recognize that the law of the military asks them to follow the orders of the person with higher rank and gives this officer absolute authority. They believe they owe absolute authority only to their conscience and to God.

There are many stories of high-ranking commanders who have ordered or implied an order that is evil and unjust. Although the military rules give some leeway about this, soldiers could be dishonorably discharged, or even jailed, for refusing to follow an order.

Conscientious objectors see that all wars are about territory, greed, and power—all of which Jesus spoke against. They don't believe it is right to kill others over boundaries, over oil, or over power plays.

The Holy War

Historically, most religions believed some wars were holy, fought for God and under God's command. Christians considered the Crusades a holy war, fought to regain the Holy City of Jerusalem. Some radical Muslims consider their war against American imperialism and American capitalism and against Jews and Christians to be a "holy" war.

While the warriors fight for what they believe is right, religious leaders the world over promote violence, either by encouraging it or through their silence. Many Christians reject the "holy war" idea, believing all wars are evil, although some may be a necessary evil that must be fought in certain circumstances.

The Just War Tradition

Christians who believe war is acceptable under very rare circumstances recognize that there are many reasons why we go to war. They determine whether or not a war is just, and only commit to a war that satisfies certain criteria.

Many Christians see war as a spectrum. On one end of the spectrum are those warriors who believe every war is just, and that they have the right to wage war under any circumstances. On the other end are those Christians who believe no war is just. The "Just War" tradition fits somewhere in the middle. The theory was first advanced by St. Augustine in the fourth century and then further developed by the Catholics. It can act as a guide for Christian lawmakers to determine when it is right to wage war, and when it is not.

The Just War theory first tries to restrict war by making it a last resort. Then it tries to reduce the horrors of a necessary war by setting limits and parameters to the damage done by the war, and creating ways to evaluate and think about war in order to stay within those limits. It insists there be a very strong reason for overriding the presumption that exists in favor of peace.

What is a Just War? In order for a war to be just, it needs to fulfill the following criteria:

1. A war is permissible only when it confronts a real and certain danger. It must address an actual violation rather than a perceived violation.[7] The Just War must not be pre-emptive or preventive. It is not a war of choice. According to this theory, we can't start a war because we think that someone, in the future, might start a war against us. However, according to this theory, a country can make a pre-emptive strike if another country's troops are at the border threatening to attack.

Although the government used the word "pre-emptive" to describe the Iraq War, many historians and diplomats do not accept this term; they see the Iraq War rather as a preventive war. There is a big difference between the two.[8] If a country's about to be attacked, and its forces counter-attack before that can happen, the war is pre-emptive. If one country believes that another country might attack sometime in the future, and the threatened country attacks first, the war is preventive. Pre-emptive war has standing in international law, because a country has a right to attack another country that threatens imminent attack. Preventive war has no standing in international law. Many countries around the world, as well as citizens within the United States (including millions of Christians), questioned the validity of the wars in Iraq and Afghanistan as preventive wars, fearing they would set a very dangerous precedent for the future.

2. In order for a war to be considered a Just War, it must be legally declared by a lawful government, not by private groups or individuals. A Just War is nation against nation; it is not a group of people against a nation, or a group of people against a group of people. Many wars are not declared by Congress, even though the Constitution says that they must be. Often they are just declared by the President. In the case of the Iraq War, Congress told the President to attack whenever he felt he should.

President Obama asked Congress to make the decision

about military operations against Syria. The Congress decided not to put boots on the ground.

The ethnic cleansing of Bosnia and Serbia and the war against the civilian population of the Sudan is not Just War; it's genocide. The 9/11 attacks, and attacks in Spain, London, Bali, Paris, Tunisia, Brussels, and other places, are not part of a Just War, because no nation sent the hijackers to attack these locations.

3. There must be a right intention. There must be a desire for a greater Good to prevail. Wars fought over territory or oil, or to keep up our standard of living, are not considered right intentions. The outcomes will not balance the deaths and maiming of hundreds of thousands, if not millions.

4. "There must be a reasonable chance of winning."[9] A Just War demands a reality check. If it will be nothing but a slaughter, with little chance of winning the peace, the war should not be declared.

5. Good must outweigh evil. "The means used in fighting the war must be proportionate to the end sought so the good which results must outweigh the evil which the war would do."[10] The damage to be inflicted and the costs of war must be proportionate to the good expected to result by taking up arms.

Soldiers must try to distinguish between armies and civilians, and never kill civilians on purpose,[11] although it's difficult to keep the bombs away from the innocents in any war. According to the Geneva Convention, carpet bombing or indiscriminate bombing that is not specifically targeted against enemy combatants is illegal. Ted Cruz has called for carpet bombing in Syria, which would cause thousands of civilians to be killed. He later refined his statement, suggesting he didn't know what "carpet bombing" was.

During World War II, millions were killed in the bombings of cities from both sides. The dropping of atomic bombs on the civilians in Hiroshima and Nagasaki still has ongoing medical consequences for those who lived through it. During the Vietnam War, there were several scandals over the killing of Vietnamese civilians. Although it's understood there are often civilian deaths as collateral damage, the Vietnam War was one of the first modern wars in which American soldiers willingly killed civilians. Both Lt. William Calley and Captain Ernest Medina were tried for the massacre of civilians at My Lai (though only Calley, who claimed he was following Medina's orders, was convicted). During that war, the U.S. government dropped tons of the defoliant Agent Orange in Vietnam. There have been continued long-term medical effects in those exposed to it.

6. The winner of the war must never require the utter humiliation of the loser. Many wars have grown out of oppression that results from the terms of peace.[12] Most historians agree that World War II grew out of the severe conditions placed on the Germans by the terms of surrender of World War I. These conditions created starvation, riots and protests, anger and frustration, and a social atmosphere that was ripe for Adolf Hitler to come to the forefront.

7. "The war must be the last resort after all other possible solutions have been tried and failed."[13] A war is never taken lightly, and the Just War tradition recognizes that other avenues must be tried, and proven to fail, before moving to war. Diplomacy is the starting point and demands a strong commitment. Sometimes the diplomatic process seems to take longer, but it's still shorter than a war.

Discerning what makes a Just War is not easy. Every country that wages war believes it is acting for the Good. During the Civil War, soldiers from both sides marched into battle with the Bible in hand, claiming that God was on their side.

In World War II, Germany, which considered itself a Christian nation, used the same justification for war that other countries, including the United States, have used. The German leaders went to war to protect the fatherland against a perceived threat to their country. They believed they had to protect the interests of their country, as well as preserve the purity of the German race against the Jews, the mentally ill, the gypsies, and the homosexuals. By declaring their race ethnically pure, they were intent on creating a paradise on earth and bringing in the thousand-year reign of their version of the Second Coming.

The Catholic catechism recognizes it's possible for us to be wrong about our motivations for going to war: "Given techniques of propaganda and the ease with which nations and individuals either assume or delude themselves into believing that God or Right is clearly on their side, the test of comparative justice may be extremely difficult to apply."[14] We are to keep a good watch over our motives, and over the reasons given for why a particular war is necessary for the "good of the state."

Even if a war is considered "just," the consequences are always horrendous. Abraham Lincoln anguished over war, recognizing that "the evils of war even in the 'best wars' . . . breathed forth famine, swam in blood, and rode on fire; and long, long after, the orphans' cry and the widows' wail continued to break the sad silence that ensued."[15] Garry Wills, in his book *Lincoln at Gettysburg*, says, "Lincoln had no illusions about war's 'nobility.' It is a cover for other crimes. And the longer it goes on, the more it outraces any rational purposes. Even noble yearnings serve savagery. . . ."[16]

The American Un-Just Wars

The Founding Fathers, in an attempt to guard against the many dangers of war, added some other limits to the tendency toward war. They wanted to make sure that the checks and balances of our government would keep any headstrong president from making executive choices without the agreement of a majority within the government. They said war must be declared by the Congress. Even so, this Constitutional law has usually been ignored and we continue to enter undeclared and ill-advised wars. The United States has taken part in about 175 wars throughout our history. Only five wars were declared by Congress—the War of 1812, the Mexican War of 1846, the Spanish-American War, World War I, and World War II. Wars *not* formally declared included the American Civil War, the Korean War, Vietnam War, Grenada, Haiti, Somalia, Bosnia, Afghanistan, and both Iraq wars.[17]

The Vietnam War violated at least six of the principles for the Just War. There was no threat to our country. Our rights had not been violated. The war was never declared by Congress. The United States had virtually no chance of success in a guerrilla war. We dropped millions of tons of bombs on Vietnam, destroyed much of the country, and killed countless civilians, and our goal was unclear.

Although some considered the Persian Gulf War (1991) a Just War, because the allies were repelling Iraq's invasion of Kuwait, there were others who did not consider it just. It wasn't a last resort. The destruction was not proportional. According to the United Nations, "the bombing reduced Iraq to near 'stone age' conditions in some places."[18]

We say we went to war in the name of democracy. But if we truly want to establish democracy in another country, we have to realize that its ideas of this form of government may not follow the principles of our own. We may not be happy with the country's self-will. Although we don't yet know how Iraq's democracy will play out over the years, the government being established there is not a true democracy because it does not protect the minority, and it is taking away some democratic laws that existed before the United States invaded. The democracy being established in Iraq gives power to the majority (the Shiites) without the protection of rights or adequate representation by the minority (the Sunnis). The rights women had under Saddam Hussein are being diminished, and, in some cases, taken away from them, which may leave women with less democracy than they had under Hussein. Although some may think this was worth fighting and dying for, a government that takes away rights from more than half of its citizens is not a democracy, regardless of what we call it.

The Iraq War bred and encouraged Al Qaeda and ISIS.

The war was justified by a lie. President Bush first told U.S. citizens there were weapons of mass destruction, which could reach us within forty-five minutes. Not true. He said this was an imminent danger even though there was no evidence of these weapons. If anything, there was evidence that they did not exist. No one could find them. Going to war for something as vague as a possibility is not sufficient justification for war. We were then told we had gone to war because Iraq was a terrorist state. But that wasn't true either. Al Qaeda was not in Iraq until we went into the country and caused so much anger that Al Qaeda saw virgin territory for its work. Since the year 2006, it has given rise to ISIS. Most of the 9/11 terrorists were from Saudi Arabia, but we never discussed going to war with that country, which is the only one that had a close connection with the terrorists.

The war has fomented terrorism. We have given Al Qaeda an extra justification for its actions, since its members can now see themselves as freedom fighters trying to repel the invaders. Insurgents have become more powerful as they battle what some see as the occupying force, and others see as the Great Satan of the West.

We were then told we had gone to war to overthrow Saddam Hussein. But international law recognizes the sovereignty of other countries. If we were to start overthrowing bad dictators, we would have a great deal of work to do. How would we decide whom to overthrow? Would we start with Amnesty International's list of the bad guys? Would we then have to continue on and depose leaders in more than a hundred countries, ranging from Albania to Burundi to Rwanda to Syria and the Sudan? If we are in the business of warring only with despots, why is it the last three wars we have had were in oil-rich countries? Why are the other despots allowed to continue their tyranny?

By no means was this a last resort. The inspectors were in Iraq. Iraq was fairly quiet. The no-fly zone and sanctions against oil, against medical equipment, against metals, and against anything that could be used to make explosives or nuclear weapons were in place. We had been bombing Iraq every week for twelve years during the Clinton administration. Iraq was not a danger to us. If anything, there was evidence Hussein was weakening, and any talk about his power was pure swagger. He was simply lying about his strength. Even after weapons of mass destruction weren't found, many Republican leaders continued to say they were still there, despite the lack of evidence. When Colin Powell discovered he had been fooled, and given the wrong intelligence, he was furious. He had been persuaded that he had the truth, when really he had been forced to give false information to the United Nations and to Congress.

What was the real reason for the Iraq War and the Afghanistan War? Certainly it had to do with our need for oil, and our need for military bases in the Middle East. We wanted to bring democracy to the Mideast, believing that the "Road to Jerusalem went through Baghdad." We believed if we could change the government in Iraq into a democracy, the rest of the countries would follow, thereby removing the funding and support for the terrorists attacking Israel. However, there was a very low possibility of actually being able to promote democracy in Iraq.

The pattern in Iraq is not new. The U.S. government

has not had quite the sterling past that we would like to think it has. Historically, our country has not always done so well at choosing which despots to support, and which not to support. We supported the Shah of Iran, Ferdinand Marcos in the Philippines, Salvador Allende in Chile, and Sukarno and then Suharto in Indonesia, and we have gone back and forth about whom to help or not to help in Central and South America. Since Christians want a larger say in the government, it might be good for us to face our past, and try to rectify some of our not-quite-so-Christian foreign policy decisions.

The Laws of War

Once a nation has entered into war, there are laws governing behavior toward civilians and prisoners, as well as the behavior of its own soldiers. Many of these laws are part of the Geneva Convention, which was signed in 1949. The Geneva Convention includes the following provisions to try to reduce the atrocities of war:

- The Geneva Convention forbids torture, mutilation, rape, slavery, arbitrary killing, genocide, and crimes against humanity, which include forced disappearance and deprivation of humanitarian aid.
- It forbids war crimes, including apartheid, biological experiments, hostage taking, attacks on cultural objects, and depriving people of the right to a fair trial.
- The Geneva Convention recognizes the difference be-

tween civilians and soldiers. For example, a civilian who shoots an enemy soldier may be liable for murder, but a soldier who shoots an enemy soldier and is captured may not be punished.

- Prisoners of war are to be treated humanely. They must not be subject to torture, or medical or scientific experiments of any kind. Many nations, including the United States, have tortured prisoners, using the rationalization that we receive important information through torture. This is questionable and has never been proven. However, according to the Christian Just War theory, torture is unacceptable for any reason and cannot be justified. Prisoners of war must also be protected against violence, intimidation, insults, and public curiosity. The public display of POWs is prohibited. However, Iran and North Korea have publicly displayed American prisoners.

- When questioned, it must be in the prisoner's native language. Prisoners of war must only give their names, ranks, birth dates, and serial numbers.

- Prisoners of war may not be punished for the acts they committed during the fighting unless the opposing side would have punished its own soldiers for those acts as well.

- There is to be no destruction of property unless justified by military necessity.

- Warring parties must not use or develop biological or chemical weapons.

When we went to war in Iraq, George W. Bush decided the United States would not follow the rules of the Geneva Convention. Instead, we would determine our own laws.

As a result, thousands of Iraqis have been detained, many in secret, in prisons in Iraq, Afghanistan, and Guantánamo Bay. Although the Supreme Court found this illegal, many prisoners still have not been released.

Particularly troubling was Mr. Bush's prisoner rendition policy. Rendition means, if we want a prisoner to be interrogated but we don't want to be the ones to torture him for information, we send him to a country that is happy to torture him for us. We can claim we're innocent of using torture as part of interrogation, but we are still coconspirators. We get around the values of democracy and Christianity by saying "it's not on our soil!" Prisoners have been sent to be interrogated in Uzbekistan, Syria, Afghanistan, and Jordan. In most cases, these prisoners had no useful information.

Whether a war is just or not, the Geneva Convention set down rules about how to treat prisoners and civilians in war. When Jesus said love your enemy and love your neighbor—even the person you hate—he was affirming that all people are God's children and are to be respected. The Geneva Convention recognizes basic human dignity as part of human rights.

It's easy to justify inhumane treatment and torture by saying we need the information these prisoners have and that this information could save lives. But who gets caught up in the net? The innocent as well as the guilty. How good is information from prisoners who have been detained for two or three or four years? Not very good at all, according to most reports.

Creating a Just Peace

Many Christians have looked not at war, but at how to keep the peace. They ask how they can actually become peace-makers through their activities. They recognize that pacifism is not passive, but active.

Quaker founder George Fox struggled with how to react as a Christian to the issue of war. He recognized Christians need to come to terms with this important topic, and this may be a long spiritual process. Fox believed that if Christians decide not to fight, then they have to work toward creating peace.

Fox said, "I lived in the virtue of that life and power that took away the occasion of all wars." Pacifist Christians recognize that almost all wars (if not all of them) begin because of unjust conditions. We sow the seeds of dissension long before they grow into conflict and war. If we can remove the conditions that cause war, peace has a chance.

The Peace Churches have held a number of Synods and Conferences aimed at creating and defining a "Just Peace" tradition in contrast to the "Just War" tradition. The churches dissent from the militaristic world view and seek a better way to resolve international conflict.

"Just Peace" is defined as "A collective and dynamic, yet grounded, process of freeing human beings from fear and want, of overcoming enmity, discrimination and oppression, and of establishing conditions for just relationships that privilege the experience of the most vulnerable and respect the integrity of creation."[19]

A Just Peace contains three steps:

- "Recognition and taking responsibility for the injustice done." A Just Peace needs to include principles of justice, equality, and fairness. Negotiations need to be mediated without the use of threats or rewards or coercion, and without exploiting what might be asymmetrical power relations. The strong side might exploit its power and the weak side might question whether anything fair and just can come out of these negotiations. Sometimes the structure of the negotiation would allow the weak side to veto ideas that might affect them unfairly. It is understood that terms need to be mutually beneficial.

  A Just Peace recognizes that war pits one side against the other and puts the blame on only one side. An awareness of injustice cultivates negative emotions such as outrage, anger, indignation, envy, resentment, depression, disappointment, humiliation, vengeance, a sense of helplessness, and all other passions that people feel when they have been deprived of their rights and basic needs. People feel powerless and humiliated by the situation, as well as by their inability to change the situation. When they are asked to work to eliminate and correct the injustice, they begin to develop the positive emotions of self-esteem, a sense of power, and pride.[20]

- The second step says that an apology and asking for forgiveness is part of the transitional phase, which refers to retributive justice, and also includes a recognition of each person's or nation's part that caused the injustice. It is recognized that the injustices of the

past need to be corrected in order to end the conflict,
stabilize peace relations, and/or secure reconciliation.
- The third step is that a Just Peace provides compensation of the victim's side, which is called "reparative or
compensating justice." It may be necessary for one or
both sides "to moderate or reduce claims of injustice,
or to be more responsive to the other's claims in order
not to endanger the peace."[21]

At times there are so many grievances and so much bit-
terness that this compensation side is delayed, so the suffering can stop and the first phase of peacemaking can
happen with compensation and reconciliation occurring at
a later time. After World War II, Western Europe was successful at establishing peace because it left aside the issue
of past injustices for the future and worked on cooperation
between the different sides of the conflict.[22]

Sometimes wars have begun because our actions have
allowed, and even encouraged, the occasion for war. We
have given arms to various countries, which have then
used them against other countries, and eventually against
us. We sold arms to Saddam Hussein to use against the
Iranians. At that time, Hussein was our friend, and we
were intent on helping him. Later, we faced those weapons
ourselves.

The same problem occurred in Afghanistan, when we
supported and trained the Afghan soldiers against Russia
and gave them the weapons they could then turn against
us. We've given arms to Syrian rebels, which then have
sometimes been used against us. We arm Israel, yet these
arms are sometimes used against Palestinian civilians.

In 2005, George W. Bush sold arms to both India and Pakistan. Since these were two countries with a long history of tensions and conflicts, we have now armed both sides of a conflict, both of whom have nuclear weapons. We shouldn't be surprised if the conflict between India and Pakistan escalates further, eventually erupting in war. We are adding fuel to the fire. Rather than working as peacemakers, we are creating the occasion for war.[23]

Trying to Diminish the Effects of War

President Barack Obama has made new choices about how to deal with international conflict, and to reduce the cost of war in both money and lives.

The Afghanistan War and the Iraq War together may end up costing 5 to 6 trillion dollars, once all the resulting medical problems are paid for. The price and consequences of these wars will go on for decades.[24] The conflict with Libya in 2011 was handled differently than these two wars. Instead of putting boots on the ground, the United States formed coalitions with other NATO countries. These countries put the focus on air power, and NATO led most of the air attacks, while the Americans took a more supporting role such as surveillance, electronic jamming, and tanker refueling. Although both U.S. and NATO officials said their mission was not to hunt, capture, or kill Qaddafi, nevertheless, they took the attitude that, "if Qaddafi should happen to be at one of those locations when the missiles strike, so be it." The cost of this conflict was relatively small by military standards: 1.1 billion dollars. No lives were lost on the

NATO side. The entire mission took nine months rather than years.[25]

Obama has increasingly relied on drones for identifying and killing prime targets. Robotic warfare eliminates the danger to soldiers on the ground and is much cheaper than war, but it does not eliminate collateral damage. It is estimated that anywhere from 5 to 50 civilians are killed for every desired target. Just like war, the effects of drone warfare can lead to the same rage, frustration, and desire for vengeance, and can motivate the victims to take revenge in whatever way is possible. Since many targets stay hidden much of the time, it is difficult to find occasions when they will be out in public. Often, they only come out for weddings and funerals, which is the reason why we often hear of entire wedding parties killed in search of one target. This makes lifelong enemies of any survivors.[26]

Giving to War Takes Away Money for Peace

War is one of the nation's most expensive undertakings. Once a war starts, more and more money is taken away from other services and diverted into arms. War is expensive. Combat pay is increased. New weapons have to be created and built and deployed. Tanks have to be built and fully armed and protected. Airplanes are shot down, and new ones are built. Imagine what that money could do if it were diverted to peacemaking and peacekeeping. Imagine how much more peacefully we could coexist in this country by investing that money in our infrastructure and in our society.

The Casualties of War

World War I killed 10 million people; World War II, 38 million. More than 100,000 were killed in a single day at Hiroshima. More than 56,000 Americans were killed in Vietnam, and there were reports that hundreds of thousands of Vietnamese, if not more than a million, were victims of that war. Besides our own casualties in Iraq and Afghanistan, hundreds of thousands of people from those countries were killed. If we could neatly keep war away from civilians, we would have a better estimate of who has been killed in combat, and would be able to limit the casualties. But that's not possible in war.

The mental and physical costs of war are also high. Soldiers and civilians are killed or wounded; rehabilitation takes months, if not years; soldiers get sick from the use of chemical and biological warfare. Their lives and the lives of their families are often ruined, as they struggle for the rest of their lives with physical impairments and mental problems. One veteran my husband and I know told us he hasn't been able to sleep since Vietnam. Another person we know ended up in jail, and told us that the mindset of war led to his illegal activities at home. Soldiers who come home from war have a higher rate of unemployment and suicide.

The harm of war does not come just from the deaths of hundreds of thousands of soldiers and civilians. Homes are destroyed. Cities are blasted. Businesses ruined. Children are unable to go out and play, because of the dangers from mines and bombs and shooting. The environment is compromised, sometimes ruined beyond any immediate repair.

How have we dealt with these problems? In many cases,

we've ignored them. For some years after Vietnam, the government refused to recognize the consequences of Agent Orange. For many years after the Gulf War, no one wanted to recognize Gulf War Syndrome. As a result of the wars in Iraq and Afghanistan, thousands of soldiers have returned with PTSD, but are not getting the help that they need. Many of them wait for help for months, some for years, and some of them die because they have waited too long.

Economic prosperity is another casualty. The Congressional Budget Office estimates that the cost of deploying the troops in Iraq was $9 billion to $13 billion; the monthly cost of the war was about $8 to $9 billion; returning the forces to the United States was about $7 billion, and the temporary occupation of Iraq would cost about $1 billion to $4 billion per month.[27]

Peacekeeping in the Place of War-Making

If we get rid of war, what do we put in its place? We know far more about peacemaking and peacekeeping than we did two or three decades ago. We have learned far more about conflict resolution, alternatives to violence, and other methods for averting war, as well as diminishing the after-effects of war. In fact, if we applied the same amount of energy, and just a portion of the money, to peace as we do to war, we could start to find ways to resolve problems without killing and destroying countries. World peace may not be around the corner, but we're never going to achieve it by going to war with every country that has oil or a despotic government. In fact, many studies of nonviolence have found that nonviolence is often just as effective, if not more so, than violence. Under those circumstances, which would we choose? There are many alternatives to war.

Historically, more than twenty countries have won independence through nonviolent means, or at least partially through nonviolence. The American Revolution began with a series of successful nonviolent protests. Before the American Revolution, the British tried to tax the colonists by introducing the Stamp Act, which taxed all printed paper, including legal papers, newspapers, cards, and pamphlets. When the ship carrying the stamps came into the Philadelphia Harbor in 1765, the city's church bells tolled all day long in protest, and the colonists' ships flew their flags at half-mast. Colonists refused to use the stamps, and by 1766, the Act was repealed.

The British then tried to pass the Townshend Acts, which imposed other unfair taxes on trade goods. Again, most of the colonists refused to buy anything that carried the tax. The names of any colonists who bought the taxed goods were published on a list as a protest against their actions. The tax was repealed, except for the tax on tea.

In 1773, when a ship came into Boston Harbor carrying tea that would be taxed, colonists threw the tea into the harbor, refusing to accept the tax. Although the Boston Tea Party is not always characterized as nonviolent protest, since property was destroyed, it is considered a form of resistance that did not lead directly to war.

Other countries have practiced nonviolent protests with great success. Pontius Pilate once brought images of Caesar into Jerusalem, even though it was against Jewish law. The Jews begged him to remove the images, but he refused. In response, the Jews camped out around his house for five days and five nights. Pilate then summoned the crowds to the stadium, surrounded the Jews with soldiers, and said that he would kill them unless they would accept these images of Caesar. As if of one mind, all the Jews fell to the ground and proclaimed they were ready to be killed. When Pilate realized he could accomplish little with the death of thousands of Jews, he removed the images.[28]

Many countries achieved their independence through nonviolence. Examples include India in 1947 (in great part through the nonviolent work of Gandhi), Poland in 1989, the Velvet Revolution in Czechoslovakia in 1989, and South Africa in 1994, when black and white South Africans were allowed to vote together for the first time.

Although the U.S. government is not a full supporter of nonviolence programs, there are a number of universities, colleges, and institutes that are studying how nonviolence can be used, and many are already using it in the world.

Many universities now have classes in conflict resolution and alternatives to violence. These include the study of how nonviolent approaches have worked throughout history, and training in nonviolent methods. There are classes and studies of how to use language to lead to reconciliation, rather than upping the ante to create more violence. Often the fires of war are stoked with bombastic threats, "us against them" thinking that has no care for the humanity of people on the other side or used as macho swagger, daring the other side to attack us. At the beginning of the Iraq War, George W. Bush said, "Bring it on." His bravado solved nothing and opened us to one of the the longest wars in our history. Most of the Republican candidates talk tough about what they would do with ISIS or with Russia or with North Korea, but this kind of talk adds fuel to the fire rather than creating an environment where peace has a chance.

Peacemaking demands knowledge, experimentation, creativity, and understanding of the situation, the culture, the language, and the root problems. It demands knowledge, training, and practice—just as war does. Like war, it sometimes teaches us to go against our natural human tendencies. War teaches a decent and peaceful human being to kill; peace training teaches people to quell their anger, to stop the rhetoric, and to try other solutions.

There is not a shortage of trained and knowledgeable people in peacemaking. There also are not quick solutions. But there are possibilities for resolving conflicts nonviolently, if the desire is there.

Peacemaking at the War College

The U.S. Army War College in Carlyle, Pennsylvania, has a Peacekeeping and Stability Institute that was created in 1993 by the Chief of Staff of the Army, General Gordon Sullivan. Sullivan recognized that the United States would be faced with peacekeeping in the future, but that there was no organization dealing with this.

I talked to Associate Professor William Flavin, who teaches peace operations at the U.S. Army War College. Flavin had been a member of the Green Berets, and most recently helped in peace-building and peacekeeping in Bosnia-Kosovo.

Flavin said the Institute presents several classes on peace operations, rule of law, and international development. These courses provide the student with the opportunity to study the rule of law, peace-building, and transition planning.

Peace programs are designed to go on before, during, and after a conflict. Flavin says, "Part of the idea is to expose everyone to each other so people can understand there are various ways of doing things. . . . We've been trying to talk about a better conceptual model for peace-building. It's true, you might have to use security forces and military forces, but the over arching objective is peace building. The evaporation of the Cold War constraints with the fall of the USSR in 1989 and the success of several UN and UN-sanctioned operations encouraged member nations to support an ambitious agenda extending UN Peace Operations to several complex crises, including Cambodia, Haiti, Somalia and the Balkans."

Flavin says, "We found that sometimes, when separating people, no one understands each other, and the separation merely postpones the understanding and postpones solving the problem. So besides separating people, we had to have some mechanism in place, as in South Africa, to create justice."

Bosnia was one of the countries where peacemaking and peacekeeping was very effective. "The European Union is now running Bosnia," says Flavin. "Originally, we thought we'd need about 600,000 troops on the ground in Bosnia and 100,000 in Sarejevo alone, based on a World War II analysis. But we only needed about 200 NATO forces." I asked Flavin whether this would work in Iraq. He replied,

"The principles of peacekeeping and peace-building are the same. There is no mystery about what should be done. But in Iraq, the process has been characterized by fits and starts. There have been at least three major phases in the process of building governance, each marked by a significant change in policy and implementation. The ad hoc and disjointed nature of these efforts exacerbated the challenge of establishing governance in Iraq. The process currently in place is the latest attempt to provide the legitimate governance."

"You have to take your time," he continued. "It is better to do this over a longer period of time, so you can gain consensus. You get people beginning to buy into things and eventually you have a working solution. If you try to force a solution there is no time to build consensus. The challenge is to convince the average citizen of Iraq, based on the disjointed nature of the previous attempts, that the current attempt at governance is legitimate and valid so consensus can be built around the peace process. The governance decisions coupled with the decision to disband the entire Iraq Army and the de-Baath policy (who were supporters of Hussein) have established conditions that have exacerbated the instability and retarded the move toward stabilization."

Using Diplomacy

Dr. Norman Graebner taught American history and American diplomacy for more than fifty years, at the University of Illinois and then the University of Virginia. He was a renowned scholar in this field. He also was my uncle, and the person to whom this book is dedicated. He clarified some of the principles of diplomacy. "My approach emphasizes diplomacy and emphasizes peace, not war," he said. "The problem occurs when people in power see America's role as to kick the world in the teeth. I see the purpose as getting along with other nations. Through diplomacy. Negotiation. With tolerance. With wisdom. When a Secretary of State goes around and tells people off, it isn't diplomacy. That's not reaching a settlement on anything. You tell them off and walk away, make believe 'I was really tough there, I'm pushing democracy!' It looks good in the press, but it's not effective."

Dr. Graebner was one of the first to teach democracy in Japan after World War II. He had to discover how to explain democracy to a country that had been ruled by an emperor. He said, "It's easy to talk about democracy, but how do you make a country democratic? Democracy is born from within, with the right leadership, the right education, the right security; you have to have a lot of things right. If a country doesn't have those things, it won't be democratic. If a country has what is right, it will have democracy no matter what the United States does or says."

Graebner was concerned about the way we become friends with a country (such as Iraq in the 1980s) and then enemies (with Iraq in the 1990s) without a consistent foreign policy. He quotes George Washington, who said in his farewell address, "The Nation which indulges toward another a habitual hatred or a habitual fondness is in some degree a slave. It is a slave to its animosity or to its affection, either of which is sufficient to lead it astray from its duty and its interest." Clearly we have been a slave to a number of countries over the centuries, moving from fondness to animosity in many of the countries where we are now fighting.

I asked him how American diplomacy is applied to such problems as war and conflicts. He answered, "The government has to think about the costs. You have to be clear about the goal, but you have to have the means to achieve that goal. You have to be willing to evaluate power carefully."

There are rules for diplomacy. "In diplomacy, there is always a quid pro quo. When dealing with someone, you always have to have something to give in exchange. Diplomacy is not demanding, it's dealing. There is always a trade-off; if not, there is no diplomacy. Otherwise, all you do is demand and you become the bully. Moralism puts an end to diplomacy."

Graebner said in order to work in the world, we have to have good relationships with other countries, for two reasons: "First of all, you may need the support of other nations if you get into trouble, and secondly, because these other nations might be right. If we believe in majority rule, when the majority of other nations are against us, they may be right. In this case, they were proven to be right."

Which Is the Party of Peace?

Neither the Democrats nor the Republicans would be considered a Peace Party. Both take strong stands on making sure the United States has a strong military.

However, President Barack Obama believes in working

diplomatic channels arduously in hopes of not having to go to war. He has been criticized for this stance by most of the Republican Congress, who think of this diplomatic stance as "weak." Under President Obama, the Unites States has ended the wars in Iraq and Afghanistan. The focus has moved to Al Qaeda and ISIS, and to preventing the spread and the use of nuclear weapons, biological weapons, and cyber security breaches. The Democrats also recognize that some of the causes of international conflicts come from climate change, which leads to scarce resources and much suffering from drought and famine and catastrophic natural disasters. They also recognize that conflict comes from unequal distribution of wealth, from lack of education, and from discrimination. Working for humanitarian causes helps make the world a more just and peaceful place. The Democrats emphasize diplomacy.

A Christian Choice

Whom do we choose—Barabbas, who was a Zealot and advocated the violent overthrow of the foreign government, or Jesus? Are we willing to love our enemies, to not seek revenge, to not pay back evil with evil, to try to live at peace with everyone? Becoming peacemakers may be a process. We may not learn it all at once. It is a radical and difficult challenge. The struggle for peace calls for discussion, listening, wisdom, and restraint. It is a Christian process that seeks methods for creating, establishing, and maintaining peace.

Although both Republicans and Democrats have voted

over and over again for war, there is a strong and emerging Christian voice that questions whether war is the best approach to resolve conflicts. To reach for peace, many Christians recognize we have to replace old ways of thinking with new visions. We have to overcome fear with hope.

There is a prayer written by a Palestinian Christian that challenges the ease with which we create enemies and divide people: "Pray not for the Arab or Jew, for the Palestinian or Israeli, but pray rather for ourselves, that we might not divide them in our prayers, but keep them both together in our hearts."[29]

Chapter Seven

Confronting Terrorism and Fear

*"For I know what plans I have for you,
Yahweh declares, plans for peace, not for
disaster, to give you a future and a hope."*
Jeremiah 29:11

Jesus told us to "fear not." He brought us a message of hope, not fear. Is this a reasonable message, considering there are threats all around us—to us as individuals, to our cities, to our nation, threats to our security and safety?

We live in frightening times. The world is still reeling from the attacks of 9/11 and of Madrid, London, Paris, Brussels, and San Bernardino, and terrified of another attack. We know our nuclear plants and our ports are not adequately protected. We go through careful and invasive searches every time we fly, knowing that someone could take a shoe bomb, or a scissors, or a pocket knife on board, and bring down another plane. We hear, almost daily, that North Korea is working to build nuclear bombs, which they may use against us or against their neighbors. We wonder if Iran will keep its side of the nuclear bargain, which many Republicans believe is a pact with the devil.

The terrorists seem to continually grow in numbers and gain more power. We hear that ISIS is active in Iraq and Syria, and seemingly almost everywhere else in the world.

We worry about our retirement and the perils of all the safety nets being removed if Social Security doesn't get fixed quickly. We see the stock market going up and down, and we wonder if we'll lose all our savings. We read about corruption in corporations, and wonder how many other businesses will fail, and how it will affect our jobs, our money, our services, our lives.

We wonder if Armageddon is around the corner, with the problems in the Middle East, with the rise of China's power, with Russia's new aggressions, with war and rumors of war, with famine and earthquakes,[1] insurrections, persecutions, calamity, and plagues,[2] hurricanes, fires, global warming—all threats of great disasters.

But a state of constant fear can be just as dangerous as being in the midst of terror. The Bible repeats, innumerable times and in many different ways, that we are not to fear and instead are to put an emphasis on trust and hope. We are to do what is right and not give way to fear.[3] We are told that there is no fear in love.[4] We are to fear no evil,[5] nor the terror of the night.[6] We are not to fear bad news,[7] or fear mortal men[8] or the sword.[9] Who or what are we to fear? Only God,[10] for those who fear him lack nothing.[11] In the midst of fear and trembling, we are to know that perfect love casts out fear.[12]

Why does the Bible kept telling us not to fear? Certainly there was as much to fear in biblical times as there is now. Enemies attacked. Women were raped. Children were massacred. Innocent men were executed by a government that oppressed its citizens daily.

Fear is a good controller of any citizenry. In an oppressive government, it's the daily threat of fear that keeps the citizens from protesting, from demanding rights, from having an uprising to change their government. Even in a democratic government, fear can control and keep us in a state of panic, so we're unable to get on with our lives.

If we give in to fear, we give over our power to others who, we hope, will make everything right. We blindly trust when we fear. We don't question the scenario described to us. We believe what the government tells us, even allowing the government to take away our rights in the name of national security.

Matthew MacWilliams is writing a Ph.D. on his studies of the personality that "lives in fear." He calls it the "Authoritarian Personality," and says that people in this category are "wary of outsiders and when authoritarians feel threatened, they support aggressive leaders and policies."[13] They are afraid of terrorism, they tend to be inflexible and rigid, and they see the world in black and white; MacWilliams sees this personality as making up a high percentage of Donald Trump's supporters. He says that when the fear instinct is activated in people who would normally not be "authoritarian," they exhibit these same qualities. Since fear is so detrimental to our country, many Christians consider Trump dangerous because he attracts people who already have this powerful fear instinct, and he pulls out that fear instinct from people who ordinarily would not be fearful.

MacWilliams also points out that the Evangelicals who follow Trump ordinarily do not attend church regularly, whereas Evangelicals who know their Bibles and are regular church attenders are speaking out more and more in opposition to Trump, because they see how poisonous fear can be. Christian are told to "fear not" and to trust in God.

During a time of fear, we mistrust our neighbors, not knowing whose side they're on, or whether their opinions will endanger us further. It becomes very important for us to know who's right—about opinions, attitudes, and actions—because it seems to be a matter of life or death. We saw fear work during the Red Scare of the 1940s and 1950s, when we feared the Communists would take over our country or drop a nuclear bomb on us. We practiced hiding under our desks at school, in case the siren went off and the nuclear bomb was on its way.

When people, or governments, can engender enough fear, they seem able to get away with anything. The fear of communism led to Senator Joe McCarthy's witch hunt for anyone who had, at one time or another, been in the Communist Party, or who knew someone who was in the Communist Party. The fear was used to build up the military-industrial complex and to overprotect ourselves, to the extent that within a few decades, we had enough bombs to kill everyone in the world many times over.[14] On both a national and personal level, the fear was insidious, changing the lives of many. People were falsely accused. Careers were ruined. It is not truthful, wise, or decent to build up false fears.

Many of us experienced the same kind of fear during the attacks of 9/11, particularly in those immediate hours after the attacks, when planes were still in the air and nobody knew how many had been hijacked. I was visiting Colorado

Springs at that time, and knew this city would certainly be a target, because NORAD, Peterson Air Force Base, Fort Carson, and the Air Force Academy were within twenty minutes of where I was staying. I grabbed my keys, got into my rental car, and drove back to Los Angeles. At times, when driving through the beautiful and isolated country of western Colorado, I thought: "If I only stay right here, without a house in sight, maybe I'll be safe." It was, indeed, a false hope.

The Consequences of Helplessness

Whether or not it's true, we feel the world is out of control, and we fear there is little we can do about it. The effects of constant fear not only give our power away to anyone who promises to keep us safe, but have caused many children and young people throughout the world to act out this fear through escaping to drugs and alcohol or sex or, at the extreme, becoming suicide bombers because they feel they live in a hopeless world where only threats and hatred seem to rule.

The Founding Fathers were particularly concerned about how fear could affect our country. They were concerned about the creation of a democratic government because democracy can easily turn to tyranny, particularly in fearful times. James Madison was concerned about any times of insecurity, because at those times the power of the president becomes greater. Checks and balances lose their place. Reasonable discourse gets lost in the angry and fearful rhetoric.

When George W. Bush told Congress, and the American people, that Iraq had weapons of mass destruction that could be turned on us, and reach us within forty-five minutes, he raised the fear level within all of us. What were we to do about it? We gave him what he asked for—the power to declare war against Iraq, whenever he wanted. Congress said yes, and the few who voted against these expanded powers, such as Bernie Sanders, were considered soft on terrorism. In retrospect, many Democrats and Republicans now believe Sanders' vote was the wiser.

Fear Thrives on Secrecy

A fearful response leads to lost freedoms. Shortly after 9/11, Congress passed the Patriot Act. This act allowed the government to snoop into which books we were checking out of the library, what we were reading on the Internet, which documents we had downloaded—all with a cloak of secrecy. We had no rights to a lawyer, no rights to due process. We could be held in total secrecy in prison, without anyone knowing where we were. We could be deported if we were under suspicion, even if we were innocent. Ben Franklin said, "Those who would trade liberty for security deserve neither." Many of the American people were willing to accept the tradeoff. The National Security Agency increased its powers—snooping on e-mail and phone calls.

In fearful times, information is not as accessible. Information is guarded and protected, partly in the interests of national security, and partly because government officials tell us they know best.

As a result, we don't know whether secret policies are effective. Has the Patriot Act truly stopped other terrorist attacks? Some say yes, some say no.

In times of fear, reason and evaluation usually are not part of the process. We feel there's no time to take a deep breath, get advice from others, think, reason, evaluate, and refrain from knee-jerk reactions. In times of fear, we are in great danger of retaliating, of allowing our vengeful nature to take precedence, of telling ourselves we have to do something fast. We lose our ability to think clearly.

The result is that fear bolsters power. We turn to our leaders to give us security, to take care of us, to not let anything harm us. We want to trust them. We want to see a show of strength, a command of the situation. When they say they're handling it, we would just as soon not know what is happening, but we believe that whatever is being done must be the right thing. We often prefer to deal with fear by putting our heads in the sand, forgetting that our little behinds are still in firing range.

Some of Donald Trump's support and the excitement over his candidacy may come because he fans the fear, and then he tells us that if we trust him, he will take care of it and no bad things will happen on his watch. Of course, many Americans would love to think this is true. But if we unquestioningly trust him, it's a way of giving our power over to somebody without any proof that the person knows what he's doing, has an effective policy, or will handle a crisis wisely.

Look at almost any tyrant and see how that person rose to power. Usually it was a time of great threat and of great despair. Before World War II, when Germany's economy was in ruin, Adolf Hitler rose to power and formed a new national identity. Hitler brought the country together again, stoked up the fear of those who were part of the Chosen Race, and created a strong defense system that could handle that threat. The country banded together, but to what end? To create divisions, worship power, and subdue or kill many of the human race who were not like them.

Out of fear, we lose our cool. We are in a state of constant panic, and have no idea what to do about it. We sometimes respond by finding safety in groups. We identify with a particular group or a particular party that believes its approach is right, and demonizes anyone standing against it. There is too much at stake to be kind and welcoming to others. We form communities, but they often are communities that bond together out of hate and fear, and lash out and attack the enemy. It is the bonding that comes from a defensive posture, ever watchful of what is "out there," rather than from a community that works together to create an effective solution.

Fight or Flight

We respond to fear in different ways. Generally we respond with some form of fight or flight.

Like many animals, some of us run the other way as fast as we can when we see a threat. If we can't run, we find other forms of fleeing. We might deny the threat to make it less real. We might say "It won't happen here," or "We have good leaders. They know what they're doing," or "It's not as bad as it seems," or "Everything will be all right."

Denial is dangerous because it allows the power of others to take over. We can easily become blindsided as we were with the costly Iraq War.

Those who don't flee out of fear often turn to fight. They become full of bravado and bluster, and let the enemy know they won't back down, they won't give up their territory, they won't be a wimp or a wuss. The fighters respond to every perceived insult, slight, confrontation, or threat. They raise the temperature. What may have started as a small Girl Scout campfire becomes a conflagration, burning others and ourselves. You only need to listen to Donald Trump for a short time to see the "fight" response at its most dramatic. He has even lashed out against the Pope, who may be one of the kindest religious leaders on earth. Some call this entertaining. But the stakes are high, and even a clown realizes it's dangerous to create chaos at a circus with its high-wire acts in constant peril and its wild animals ready to attack at the slightest provocation.

This stance raises the stakes of the fight. If one person starts the battle by holding one rock, the other has to have two. If one has a hundred bombs, the other has to outdo him with two hundred. We arm ourselves to the teeth and let the other side know that we're going to get them, which leads to the other side, out of necessity, arming themselves. We demand an "eye for an eye," but soon all we have are two blind soldiers.

The fighting stance has nowhere to go except out of control. There is no evaluation, because that would mean someone would need to back down, regroup, and rethink. It is said that the first thing to go in war is "The Plan." The response will always be unpredictable. Once we begin, there is no wiggle room for us to take another approach, to try another tactic, to see if we can negotiate or reach some agreement.

To keep the hatred at a high pitch, we have to objectify the enemy, making them less than human. We demonize the enemy, calling the leader of the country "another Hitler, another Stalin, the Great Satan, the evil empire, the axis of evil." Once we do that, there is no room for discussion or debate.

If the government doesn't act quickly enough in asking for arms, firepower, airpower, or boots on the ground, it is severely criticized even though we could quickly be pulled into another unwinnable war.

The Hebrew Scriptures are filled with stories of battles and wars and the desire to defeat the enemy. The Psalmists ask God to come and heap burning hot coals on the enemy, or to protect them against the wrath of the enemy by delivering the enemy to Hell (in one form or another).

The Gospels and Epistles have none of these stories, even though Rome was the occupying power and was a cruel and ruthless nation. What did Jesus do? He told the Truth. He forgave. He healed some of the Romans when they asked, and let his Light shine to change hearts and minds.

What are we to do? Is there an alternative to fighting or fleeing?

Recognizing Our Vulnerability

Americans are constantly being told we are the richest and most powerful nation in the world. As a result, we can easily believe we are invincible, that nothing can touch us, that we're strong enough to fight back against anything. But we're not.

The Bible frequently harps on the fact that we're helpless and dependent creatures. It uses a number of metaphors to describe who we are, and many of them are metaphors of the helpless—that we are the lost sheep who are in need of a shepherd,[15] that we are to be like little children,[16] that we might be the person who has fallen among thieves, in need of a Good Samaritan to help us.[17] Sometimes God compares Himself to the poor and vulnerable and small. He is like the widow who searches for a lost coin.[18] He is like a hen that gathers her little chicks together against the threat.[19] Ultimately, He is the Son who was an itinerant preacher, with little money, who was beaten and killed by the religious authorities and the authorities of Rome. The crucifixion leaves us with an image of Jesus that truly is vulnerable and helpless and even seemingly defenseless.

Learning to accept our vulnerability allows us to put our trust in God. We learn we can't do it by ourselves. We are in need of a Savior.

Although we may pay lip service to this idea, we don't like the feeling. Part of our defensive posture comes from a belief that somehow, if we're strong enough, and have a big enough army, and spend enough money on defense, we need never believe our human condition is one of vulnerability.

If we started with an understanding of our vulnerability, our responses might be quite different from the immediate knee-jerk response we usually have when threatened by the Other.

Dealing with the Terrible Neighbor

We gain strength knowing that God is on our side. Not our side as Americans, or because we think that we're right and therefore God is on our side and not on the other person's; but knowing that God is within each one of us, guiding us with loving responses rather than hateful ones, showing us that God is on everyone's side.

When we change our perspective of others from enemies to neighbors, the relationship between us begins to change. In a sense, we are much the same as the neighbors. Usually, they have concerns similar to ours. They too want justice, freedom from oppression, and the freedom to live good lives. How they, and we, go about achieving these things may be drastically different, or they may be much more similar than we think.

The Bible has a great understanding about the enemy, some of it contrary to how we think the world actually works. We believe we best deal with enemies by keeping them in their place, never letting an ounce of love or understanding or compassion come between us and them. They are, and must remain, totally evil.

Of course, our enemies are not letting any love and understanding come from their side either. But that's the point Jesus made. He said if you love people who love you, it isn't anything extraordinary; everyone does that.[20] Christians are asked to go another step: to love their enemies.[21] Loving enemies seems to be impossible unless we decide to try it. It's a radical message, yet that's what we're commanded to do—to treat everyone as the neighbor, and to love them. How are we able to do this impossible task?

By the work of the Holy Spirit!

We can start loving our enemies by recognizing we have no choice in the matter. If there's a mad dog in the neighborhood, we can't ignore it. If there are threatening neighbors, we have no choice. We have to deal with them. We move from denial of the problem to looking clearly at the reality of the situation. The immediate response may be "Bad people, let's get rid of them!" As Christians, we need to guard against this. It's not unusual to get rid of one neighbor, only to have someone worse come in instead. In that situation, the problem hasn't really gone away. It's just gone to another neighborhood.

We first must recognize the danger to be addressed. What is the threat? Where is it coming from? How bad is it? There is no denying there are true threats, of terrorism, war, killings, and various forms of mayhem. This isn't just a threat to us in the United States; it's a threat to the world. It can kill hundreds, thousands, or millions. The threat will stop at nothing. It affects us all. We can't ignore it, deny it, or pretend it won't happen to us. We still must protect our property and our citizens.

We can begin working with the threat by working to dissipate the danger, not add fuel to the fire. We don't appease the terrorists, but we need to clearly understand the threat and let wise heads prevail. We can't get sidetracked about it. Responding with fear and trembling, and giving power away to the government, is not the answer.

Unfortunately, that's the first response we usually have to the war on terror—we get sidetracked. We get trigger-happy. We change our focus. We look the other way. After 9/11, we were of one mind with much of the rest of the world—we had to face the terrorists and we had to do it together because it affects all our neighborhoods. We recognized that there were terrorists in many countries, and if we shared information, worked together, and established a common goal, maybe we could effectively diminish, or even remove, the threat.

But we didn't do that. Instead, we started shooting at the wrong targets. We got confused about who was doing what to whom. The terrorists came from Saudi Arabia, and we decided to shoot at Afghanistan. That might have worked—if the problem had been defined as the oppressive rule of the Taliban. But that wasn't the problem; the problem was terrorists. Not only did we not stop the terrorists, we weren't even truly successful with Afghanistan. The Taliban grew in power. The elections were corrupt. We spent a lot of money, bombed many places, and killed a number of people—but we didn't solve the problem.

We then went into Iraq, a country that had nothing to do with 9/11. We spent a lot of money, bombed a lot of places, killed a lot of people—but we never defined the problem and, therefore, we never solved it. In fact, we made it worse. Al Qaeda, which had not been in Iraq, found fertile soil there. ISIS grew directly from American policies in Iraq and then spread to Syria and other countries.

If we can't define the problem, we can't solve it. Many say, "It's the Muslims!" No, that's not a clear definition of the problem. It's a particular group of Muslims. Just as I wouldn't want to be put into the same category as some Christians, most Muslims wouldn't want to be put into the category of the terrorist Muslims.

The Koran calls on Muslims to be peacemakers and not

to hate. "Be upright for Allah, bearers of witness with justice, and let not hatred of a people incite you not to act equitably."[22] There are plenty of verses within the Koran about justice and mercy, which, like many verses in our Bible, are being misinterpreted to justify hate and war and killing of the innocent.

Know Your Neighbor

Unfortunately, we know very little about the enemy we're fighting, nor do we seem to want to know, since that means recognizing their motivations. It's like having a neighbor down the street who spends a lot of time in his basement, exhibiting some occasional strange behavior, and there's no Neighborhood Watch to keep an eye on him. We need to know our enemy, and also know our neighbor!

This is not a war against a country. Terrorists live and work in more than sixty nations, on every continent. Bombing one country after another is not going to solve the problem. Deposing one bad leader after another will not solve the problem. We need to start asking what's really happening here. What's beneath the surface of these events?

Nobody does evil acts just because they woke up that morning and decided to do evil acts. After 9/11, one of my graduate-school teachers asked the question, "Why do they hate us so?" Some would answer "Because they're evil," or "Because they hate Christians and Jews," or "Because they have no respect for human life," or "Because they are jealous of capitalism." These are made-up, superficial reasons. They tell us virtually nothing about the real reason. We have to go deeper than this to solve this problem. Why do they hate Christians and Jews? Why would they be jealous of capitalism? Since they say they're doing it for God, then in their own eyes they aren't evil, any more than we consider ourselves evil for going to war.

Most of us know virtually nothing about the Middle Eastern culture and about the Muslim religion. We know very little about jihad, or what it means to fight a holy war, or why they're fighting it, or why they're fighting it now.

Unlike many Europeans, who do more traveling to other countries, many Americans have very little experience with cultures abroad. People and cultures and religions are not the same. If we assume that everyone thinks the same way that we do—about democracy, about civil rights, about what's best for a country's citizens, about religion—we provide the first spark in the powder keg of misunderstanding.

To understand other cultures, we also need to recognize that our culture is not a perfect one with such high values that every right-thinking person from another country wants to be Americanized.

There are those who truly hate the values of the West. We presume our values are the best values, but a number of other cultures find us far too materialistic—with far too much focus on making money and having money. They see us as dogmatic and self-righteous. They see our families and communities as fragmented. They can't figure out why we love guns so much, and why we don't try to stop the mass shootings. They read the papers to know that even our Christian religious groups have divisions. Some can barely talk to each other. Some of my European friends ask me, "Why are your presidential campaigns so nasty?

Why does everyone say they're Christian and then tear each other down?" We export our values throughout the world, beaming them into people's television sets every night. But there are many cultures that feel oppressed by our constant presence.

If we believe America is perfect, it will be impossible for us to listen to and comprehend any other position. If we're open to hearing the other side, we gain knowledge that can be helpful in fighting terrorism and turning the enemy into at least a neighbor, if not a friend.

Where do we find out about Muslim motivations? From Muslims. After the bombing in London, and after the arrests in the city of Leeds, several Muslim youths were shocked, although not completely surprised, that their friend, Shehzad Tanweer, was one of the suicide bombers. They explained how they understood his motivation: "He was sick of it all, all the injustice . . . why, for example, don't they ever take a moment of silence for all the Iraqi kids who die?"

Another friend of the suicide bomber called it a "double standard." "I don't approve of what he did, but I understand it. You get driven to something like this, it doesn't just happen." Many of his friends shared the same sense of outrage, of siege, of otherness, the sense that Muslims were "helpless before the whims of greater powers." In each case, none of the youths condoned the behavior, but they understood the anger that comes from people who feel wronged.

This is what the fighting stance does. It pushes those who feel defeated and alienated over the edge, and they come back with some underhanded tactic, doing what they can do to win. Terrorism is the cheapest form of warfare—

no army, little equipment, lots of attention, lots of bang for very little money. They bomb the subways and trains in Madrid and London, they blow up the buildings in New York and Washington, they blow up planes, trains, and automobiles, and resorts and nightclubs. We have been warned, from the story of David and Goliath,[23] that the little guy can stand up to the big guy, and sometimes the little guys win, or at least they can keep the big guy on edge for a long period of time. And the little guys don't go away.

How are we to deal with terrorists, without demonizing them or being naive about them, and without making matters worse?

Dining with Sinners

Suppose we looked at the example of Jesus. What did Jesus do when dealing with sinful people? In many instances, he began by asking questions, by accepting and respecting the Other, by peering into the heart of the Other. He saw their true situation, whether seeing how the poor were in bondage or how the rich were in bondage. He saw their hurt, their pain, their misery, their oppression. He saw their hypocrisy, their vengeful spirit, their judgmental natures. He didn't excuse the sin, but he dealt with the person. He understood.

He looked into the real meaning of the event. In many instances, people told Him their interpretation of an event. He spoke to the blind man, who said the reason he was blind was probably because of his own or his parents' sins. Jesus said that wasn't true, and explained the real reason—

it was so God could do His work.[24] He was told not to pick corn on the Sabbath, and was told the reason—because the Scriptures say so. He replied, "No, the Sabbath was made for man, not man for the Sabbath."[25]

Jesus peered deeply into the meaning of the event, without accepting what it looked like on the surface. He didn't accept the first knee-jerk interpretation. Nor did he accept the interpretation that always put the worst light on the action. Things weren't always what they seemed.

Jesus also went a step further, by becoming involved with others. Instead of removing Himself from sinners and outcasts, he ate with them. He dined with prostitutes and tax collectors, with fishermen and with women. He was willing to relate closely with others, even the outcasts. He was willing to continue the dialogue.

Can we get anywhere if we refuse to talk with, and dine with, sinners? Without some kind of discussion, there is no possible way that we can understand motivation, reasoning, or what the problem is. Nor can we start to develop bonds of trust and understanding if we refuse to be in the same room as our enemies. We cut off communication with whomever we consider our enemies—such as North Korea and Iran—and we even alienate ourselves from our friends, if they don't agree with us.

We might feel that the Other is impossible to love, understand, or care about. We might feel we must put our Christian values aside, and decide this problem is simply too great and our loving religion not practical. But if Christianity isn't practical in the worst of circumstances, it's no better than any religion that serves us only when things are going well. Jesus was practical. He was involved with society. As Christians, we have to take His insights and advice seriously.

Last Act Ethics

The Quaker author Dr. William Durland uses a term called "last act ethics." It means we tend to make a judgment on someone's last action, rather than going to the root cause. If someone sets a bomb, we then create all of our ethical responses based on the bombing, not on what has gone before. We don't want to deal with the whole action, but only with the most dramatic part of the action.[26] Durland says, "Last Act Ethics . . . means that we tend to hold the person who commits the last sinful act in a chain of sinful acts . . . responsible for the entire progression of wrong-doing."[27] Since the action that is most apparent is clearly wrong, we make a judgment about it and feel good about ourselves. We know evil when we see it, and set ourselves up to be able to call it correctly. Of course, the other side is doing the same thing. They see our evil, call it as they see it, and then respond. Then we do it back—they shoot, we shoot back. They bomb, we bomb back. They're evil. We are simply getting rid of the evil.

Jesus saw cause and effect another way. Rather than looking at the end result, he saw there are chains of events that lead to sin, and the last person may not be the one who most deserves punishment. When Jesus saw the adulterous woman who, we are told, was caught in the act,[28] Jesus knew that her sin was not her sole responsibility. He must have noticed the man was not around to be punished, even though adultery can't be done alone. She was not punished, only told to sin no more.

The Bible tells us "what you sow you shall reap."[29] True, to some extent. But Jesus broke the chain that said everything in life is based on cause and effect. He brought grace into the equation. Grace does not depend on what we deserve, but is a gift.[30] Durland calls grace "an immense gift that God gives us to change the state of things before our very eyes and to revolutionize history. Grace breaks the chain of everlasting cause and effect and is, in a sense, an in-breaking of God into history. It means God is everlastingly kind, even to those who do bad acts."[31]

We might feel a sense of estrangement from God, because of our "fallen" nature. If we have been given grace, by getting not our just deserts but good deserts instead, then we are asked to treat others with the grace that we have been given. We are asked to be generous. Rather than being judgmental, we are asked to forgive others as we have been forgiven.

Jesus told us that before we judge others, we need to look at ourselves. This is good advice for us as individuals and as a country. We can begin by looking at those elements of our own behavior that set up the occasion of wars, and that set up unjust situations. We are not wholly innocent here. Although some people seem to be against soul-searching and think we're soft if we look at ourselves, Jesus made it very clear that this is exactly what we're supposed to do. We are to look at our own behavior and take the log out of our own eye before peering at the speck in the other person's eye, and make repentance if necessary. By looking at ourselves, we might also get a better understanding of the Other. We might learn a little humility. If we and the Other are so much alike in our evil, perhaps we might also be somewhat alike in our goodness.

We Don't Do It Alone

The United States sometimes seems to have a cowboy mentality. I live in the West, and I love much about the cowboy culture, but there is a part of this culture, often seen in the old Westerns, that believes in the rugged individualism of the Lone Ranger who shoots all the bad guys and saves the American way of life. We sometimes forget that even the Lone Ranger didn't work alone—he had his faithful companion, Tonto, by his side. Americans have a history of being self-sufficient and self-reliant. We believe reliance on others shows our weakness.

Rather than recommending rugged individualism, the Bible emphasizes community, the bonds of working together, the importance of banding together and helping each other. The early Christian Church became powerful because of the strength of the community. Its members supported each other, guided each other, and were eventually able to destroy the oppression of Rome.

After 9/11, we banded together into a world community, creating a coalition against terror. Colin Powell sought support from all over the world, including from organizations such as NATO, the United Nations, the European Union, and the Organization of the Islamic Conference, for the fight against terrorism. In spite of the grief I shared with our nation, I also experienced a sense of power and hope, feeling we had become "one world" and it was possible to resolve this problem—together.

But we didn't follow the policy of coalition-building. Instead, we returned to the individualism that says we'll do it alone. Rather than listening to the wisdom of others, we vilified them if we didn't agree with them, and chose not to talk to them.

From the Three Rs to the Four Rs

It is possible to overcome our fear and to deal with terrorism in an effective and Christian way. We can move from the evils of revenge, retribution, and retaliation to the good of repentance, reconciliation, rehabilitation, and restitution.

It is natural for us to want revenge when we've been wronged. We easily turn to retaliation—do unto them as they have done unto us. We only need to look at the history of the world to realize this has not been totally effective. The biblical standard asks us, in most instances, to take the opposite actions.

My career consultant, Judith Claire, taught me a process to use whenever I had wronged another, or been wronged. She said, "First think about your part in it. If you wronged someone else, why did you do it? Did you do something to cause this response?" We are not to think about our actions in order to justify them, but in order to understand them so we don't do them again. Then, we are to repent and make amends. I have a great respect for people who apologize, although it is sometimes looked at as "eating crow" or being weak.

After we apologize, we try to make it right, in whatever way possible. We reconcile with the other by asking for forgiveness, and asking what we can do to reconcile. This might include restitution—doing something to make up for past wrongs; repairing the damage; giving a gift to try to bring us back into a loving relationship.

Judith recommends, "Ask yourself what was your part in this process. Was there an old grievance that didn't get resolved? Had something been simmering for some time that you ignored? Even if their response to you was out of proportion to what you had done, still, look at your own part in it first."

If we have been attacked and the proportion of the attack against us seems greater than the proportion of the wrong we have done, we still need to look at our part in it. Most terrorism comes from grievances in the past about what has been done to create an unbalance or an injustice. Sometimes the lashing out from terrorists is not specific— it seems as if the rage will lash out at anyone. Sometimes it is very specific—what you did to me, I'll do back to you at a similar target.

Beyond "Tit for Tat"

There is another way of responding, which is not tit for tat. We usually believe in tit for tat; doing the same to enemies that they did to us. Of course, a case can be made that we've overdone our part of the equation. Nineteen hijackers killed more than 3,000 innocent people on 9/11. We have now killed far more than that in Iraq and in Afghanistan, even though neither country was behind those attacks. Tit for tat usually gets out of hand.

There is another approach, called tit-for-two-tat, which has been developed by game theorists who look at how to win against aggression.[32] Robert Axelrod discusses this theory in his book *The Evolution of Cooperation*. Instead of aggressively responding in kind, we respond to defuse the situation. This doesn't mean we don't respond, but we give them an opportunity to "take it back" or to change their behavior. Coalition-building is an example of not responding in kind, but rather responding with a nonaggressive though potentially effective stance. If that doesn't work, rather than upping the stakes by responding with more force, we diminish our response, always coming in with a less aggressive stance or an equal stance.

There are other possible responses. We might also respond not with hate, but with love and compassion in a way that gains the goodwill of most of the people. Though we recognize that there will always be evil in the world, we can help diminish its power.

What would have happened if we had helped the Afghans rebuild their country rather than diverting our attention to Iraq? What would have happened if we had made a genuine effort to help the Iraqis living under an oppressive rule? What would happen if we spent our money rebuilding countries and bringing justice, rather than continuing an endless cycle of bombing, propping up leaders that countries don't want, and interfering with their internal policies?

Casting Out Fear with Hope

The alternative to fear is hope. Not unrealistic hope, or Pollyanna hope, or denial of the reality, but a vision. The Bible is filled with verses about the necessity, and the greatness, of hope over fear. We can practice hope, live hope, respond with hope. Hope sees potential. Hope changes our stance. Rather than becoming immobile out of fear, we become actively creative out of hope.

Quakers like myself believe there is "that of God" in everyone, and when we relate to another person, we look for the glimmer of God. We have found, throughout our history, that this belief has enabled us to relate to others who are considered the no-hope people, those who have been written off as "impossible," "not worth it," and "less than human."

In the early days of our country, when other settlers were warring with the Native Americans, and were being attacked and killed, their houses burned down and their children kidnapped, the Quakers were on friendly terms with the Native Americans. The Native Americans babysat the Quakers' children when the parents had to be away from home. The Native Americans had an agreement among themselves— not to attack a Quaker home or to shoot a Quaker.

Why this difference? The Quakers always treated the Native Americans fairly. They paid for the land they wanted, rather than just taking it. They signed treaties with the Native Americans, which are some of the few treaties in our history that were never broken. They never locked their doors, so the Native Americans felt welcome in Quaker homes. They respected the ways of the first inhabitants. Likewise, when other missionary groups have been kicked out by repressive governments, Quakers have often been allowed to remain.

Responding to fear through hope and respect and trust is not often a natural response. It is a learned response. But Quakers have proven that it is possible to treat the enemy humanely, not by colluding with the enemy, but by listening, reflecting, and trying to set policies in place that have a better chance of remedy and reconciliation than do more labeling, more anger, more hatred, more shooting, more war, more deaths, and another cycle of anger, hatred, war, and death. Hillary Clinton says, "We have to reject fear and instead choose resolve. . . . America's open, free, tolerant society is described by some as a vulnerability in the struggle against terrorism. But I actually believe it's one of our greatest strengths. It reduces the appeal of radicalism and enhances the richness and resilience of our communities."[33]

Hope trusts and believes that when we work together, something larger than each one of us gets created. If we only surround ourselves with like-minded people, it's easy for us to become unyielding in our "right-ness" and the enemy's "wrong-ness." We do what's been done before. We think someone else can fix everything for us. We begin to look for others who agree with us, so that our combined, powerful voices can drown out other answers. We become blinded to the possibilities that others can bring.

Hope is different. Hope believes in alternatives. It respects others and encourages everyone to think creatively, listen, and brainstorm. It believes in God's impossibilities.

Working Together

Bill Clinton ran for president as the "man from Hope" (both the town in Arkansas and the idea), and he emphasized the possibilities. John Edwards, in his speech at the 2004 Democratic convention, said, "Hope is on the way!" It was said of John F. Kennedy's presidency that "hope was in the air."[34] Barack Obama's 2008 campaign talked about hope and change. What is the hope that the Democrats speak about, versus the fear that is so prevalent with the Republicans?

The Democrats see there is hope if we rebuild our alliances so that we are, once more, working together.

Changing the Reaction

We live in a dangerous world. We live in a flawed world. There is plenty of sin on all sides. And we are always in danger of responding to any threat from our worst side, not our best. When an injustice has been done to us, we need to make sure we don't become like one of "them," and become part of the vengeful cycle of hatred. James Wallis, author of *God's Politics*, says, "We should respond out of our deepest values, not the terrorists'."[35] We need to learn not to bypass the wisdom that comes from fear, but to surrender to trust, be willing to bring love and compassion into our responses and to believe in the leading of the Holy Spirit.

Chapter Eight

Secrets, Lies, and Deceptions

"You will not spread false rumors. You will not lend support to the wicked by giving untrue evidence. . . . you will not pervert the course of justice."

Exodus 23:1–2

The nature of politics often seems to be about lies, deceptions, and "spin." Politicians do it to win elections. The media do it because hyperbole attracts an audience. We believe the deceptions because we can't believe that the nice guy from our party could possibly lie, although we can easily believe it about the other guy from the other side. Depending on which side we're on, it always seems the other side gets away with everything, while even the littlest flaw from our side is made into a glaring sin, capable of erasing any good that has ever been done.

There are always plenty of lies in politics, on both sides. But lies need to be addressed—on whichever side they happen. The media have not been helpful and honest about this. They have not always asked the hard questions or ex-

plored, fully, the deceptions. And the cost of these deceptions has been enormous.

Why are lies so dangerous? We base most of our choices
and our actions on the truth. We get married because we
believe the person is telling the truth when he or she says, "I
love you." We take a job based on a contract that we believe
to be true. We vote for candidates because we believe the
candidates are promising what they can deliver, are truthful about their stands on an issue, and are who they say they
are. When we are wrong, bad things happen to us personally and to our country. We discover that our Social Security
check has been reduced; we find out that the Peace candidate has started a long and costly war; we discover that services have been cut in our neighborhood because the new
president has just passed a bill that works against us, even
though he insisted that our lives would be better, if only he
were elected. Lies are a distraction and a detour from what
really matters.

A continuing theme in the Gospels and Epistles is the
need to call each other to account. We are to speak the
truth. Our "yes" is to be a "yes," our "no" a "no."[1] No lying.
No covering up. No trying to get away with anything or put
the blame somewhere else. We are to bear witness.

Politics and the Truth

Unfortunately, truth is something not often valued in politics. The end is often seen as justifying the means—even if
there are lies along the way. Winning is valued at any cost,

including the cost of a lie. The perception of being truthful and right is valued, even if the perception is wrong.

Republicans and Democrats alike get caught up in their lies and deceptions. Sometimes they get away with it, and sometimes they don't. It is particularly difficult to respect those who are supposed to abide by the truth when they call themselves Christian, and then, together with other conspirators, hide, obfuscate, and deny their lies.

We don't have to look far to see the many lies in government, nor their tragic consequences. Richard Nixon lied about Watergate and brought down his whole government, with forty government officials and members of Nixon's re-election committee convicted on felony charges. Lyndon B. Johnson ran on a peace ticket in 1964 at the same time he was planning on increasing the American troops going into Vietnam. Ronald Reagan either lied about or managed to have plausible deniability about the trading of guns for hostages during the Iran–Contra affair. George Herbert Walker Bush promised "no new taxes" during his election campaign, and as soon as he got into office, he raised taxes. Bill Clinton lied about his affairs, including his affair with Monica Lewinsky, and was impeached for it, although not found guilty. George W. Bush lied to the world, claiming Saddam Hussein had weapons of mass destruction, which he didn't, and led us into a long and expensive war. Barack Obama had been a constitutional lawyer but during his time in office, Edward Snowdon discovered that the National Security Agency had been doing a lot of snooping into people's personal phone calls and e-mails that seemed to be outside the limit of the Constitution.

Some explain away the lies, saying our leaders can't tell the truth because of "national security," and we simply must trust them. Lying, and not sharing important classified information because of national security, are two different things. Any president has the right not to tell truly secret information to the public, although how much needs to be secret from the Congress may be another story.

We prioritize our lies. We vote according to what we consider the worst kind of lie and who we consider the worst liar.

What's the problem with lies? Why is it so important, as a statement of Christian values and as a statement of our commitment to truth, justice, and freedom, that our leaders tell the truth?

Truth Matters

The eighth commandment is clear about lying: "Thou shalt not bear false witness."

Lies come in many forms. There are the big and small deceptions; the half-truths, the full lies, and the little white lies. There are the refusal to tell the truth; the obfuscations, the denial; clouding over, covering up, embellishing the truth; the spin; the dirty tricks and dirty gimmicks; the lies of omission and commission, and the fudging of facts. There are hypocrisy, name-calling, unfair labeling, backpedaling, flip-flopping, pulling the wool over our eyes, and the Big Pretend of righteousness. There is blindness to what is really going on, and there is a lack of integrity in not calling a lie a lie.

The Big, Fat Whopper of a Lie

Some lies are so big and so outrageous that we tend to believe that they're true because they are usually supported by some facts and declaimed with such confidence and force that we go along with them. They pull the wool over our eyes, and we don't realize we can't see clearly. Decisions are made, many times nationally or internationally, because of these lies, and the consequences are ongoing and tragic.

The two biggest whoppers in my lifetime were Watergate and the Iraq War. In the early 1970s Richard Nixon looked directly into the camera to tell us that whatever was going on he didn't know about, as, one by one, the dominoes in his government fell and the truth slowly came out, thanks to the stick-to-it-iveness of reporters Bob Woodward and Carl Bernstein.

As a result of this whopper of a lie, the nation's trust in the leadership of our government and in our ability to elect good leaders was crushed. The Watergate revelations ushered in a sense that politics was dirty and corrupt, even in our own country. It was a chaotic and distrustful time, and we probably have not yet recovered as a country.

As a result of Watergate, I personally switched political parties and began to distrust leaders in government as well as Americans' ability to discern good leaders from bad leaders. For the first time, as a young woman, I began to recognize the corruption, the dirty tricks, the hypocrisy that can be prevalent in government. Although one might say that we need to lose our political innocence at some point, it is truly a shock when it happens because we tend to believe that America is great, and our entire country let us down.

The lie about the Iraq War was supported by so many facts. I saw the trucks and the yellow dust and information about the weapons of mass destruction. Secretary of State Colin Powell, one of the most respected government leaders, told me that was all true. I felt that rousing power that comes when the bombs begin to fall and America looks so powerful and so right. It was all untrue.

Not only did this lead to such a horrible, long-lasting, expensive war, but it was truly a sin to lie to Colin Powell and to make him lie to the American people! That kind of integrity should never be compromised, and it was a terrible abuse of Powell's fine reputation.

The Republican candidates are in the process of disseminating another whopper of a lie. They are lying to us about the dangers of immigration, about the floods of Mexicans coming into our country, "raping our women, dealing drugs, and committing theft and murder." This problem is "so bad" that we have to spend billions on a wall between the United States and Mexico in order to keep these people out, even though there are now the same number of Mexicans leaving as arriving. The next part of the lie is truly silly, but is said with such confidence that many Americans nod their heads when Trump says, "The Mexicans will pay for our wall."

With this whopper of a lie, Donald Trump has actually created a lie that is multi-layered. He is over-promising and therefore will not be able to deliver on this policy. He is name-calling and labeling, which is another form of a lie; his generalizations are simply not accurate about the character and characteristics of the people coming into this country. Twenty percent of immigrants work in professional and managerial positions, and there is no more crime from any of the immigrants than there is from anyone else in this population.

Trump also adds hypocrisy to these lies, since two of his wives are immigrants. They did not come into the U.S. as criminals but as models. Trump certainly would want to keep his wives in this country and wanted them to have a path to citizenship, which they followed sometime after the marriages. He would want his family to be together and not have his children deported nor have people questioning their citizenship—and yet he supports breaking up the families of illegal immigrants who have children born in the United States.

Trump has hired illegal immigrants to build his casinos, yet he wants to make sure no one else hires them. He wants something for himself that he's not willing to give to another. Hypocrisy is being two-faced, and it tells us immediately that the person won't be fair or just in other policies.

A Little More About Hypocrisy

Hypocrites can be defined as people who have a double standard—a lower one for themselves, and a higher one for other people. They see the speck in the other person's eye, but not the big log in their own.

Jesus' main problem with the religious authorities of his day was their judgment, self-righteousness, and hypocrisy.[2] These are part of the character of Pride, considered the greatest of the Seven Deadly Sins. Those who are prideful set themselves up as gods. They stop listening to others, because they don't believe anyone else has any Truth to share. Instead of humility, they have confidence in their own perfection and think they have all the answers.

Hypocrisy confuses us. Whenever anyone proclaims his or her Christianity too loudly, we need to be suspicious. Some believe Christian values lie only on their side. This is a dangerous stance for any person, or any party, to take. It is tempting to believe this, but is it accurate?

Hypocrisy demands that we put our trust in someone who is not trustworthy. It asks us to be two-faced and not to notice the contradiction in the talk or the action. The Republican Party asks for limited government, a government that does not snoop into our lives, that allows us freedom of enterprise and freedom to fulfill our dreams, and that wants us to be prosperous. Republicans want to peer into our bedrooms and into our bodies to see if the women are pregnant and what they are going to do about it. In the most private part of a woman's life, the Republicans want power over her.

They say they want equality and freedom for America's citizens, but they don't want women to have equal pay for equal work. They don't want to grant LGBTs equal rights, and some of their candidates call minorities nasty names.

The Republicans take a strong stand on absolute adherence to the U.S. Constitution, yet they want to delay the appointment of a new Supreme Court Justice for a year or more, even though it's the President's responsibility to nominate and the Senate's responsibility to hold a hearing. The delay would leave the ninth chair of the Supreme Court unoccupied for well over a year. It would keep some important cases from going to the Supreme Court, and it would deadlock some cases with a 4-to-4 vote. That would send those cases back to the lower courts, which would prevail, even though the lower courts' findings may have been unconstitutional.

There are often very subtle forms of hypocrisy. Donald Trump doesn't drink alcohol, yet he created the Trump Vodka, which encourages others to drink. It didn't sell very well, but it was alcoholic! Mike Huckabee, who says he is for democracy, also said, "If you know someone that's not going to vote for me, let the air out of their tires Saturday."[3] Donald Trump says he is a great defender of the Constitution and democracy, but he proposes to administer an unconstitutional religious test to make sure Muslims don't come into the country. All the candidates except Bernie Sanders are Christian. Yet the Republican field—the side that gets the most Evangelical votes—has displayed as much nastiness, mud-slinging, bragging, name-calling, finger-pointing, and verbal attacks as any presidential campaign in the past. As of March, 2016, John Kasich is the only Republican candidate who has stayed above the fray.

Dirty Tricks and Dirty Gimmicks

The dirty trick is an underhanded scheme that the candidate hopes won't be exposed, although the negative consequence cannot be repaired. There's no chance for restitution and, in many cases, no chance for reconciliation. In the 2016 Republican campaign, Ted Cruz has been the master of the dirty trick. On the day of the Iowa Caucus—perhaps the most important voting since it begins the whole voting season—Ted Cruz distributed information claiming that Ben Carson would stop campaigning after Iowa and that he had an important announcement to make that week, so Carson's supporters should vote for Ted Cruz. Cruz managed, with this unethical behavior, to pull off a multi-layered lie. It was misleading. It implied that Ben Carson was dropping out of the race, and it urged voters to vote for Cruz rather than wasting a vote on Carson. It was also worded in a way that gave him deniability, which is a particularly subtle part of this lie—it implies rather than saying anything outright. He then put the blame for all his dirty tricks on his communication manager and fired him, although he didn't fire him until several weeks later, and Cruz would have had to approve these kinds of dirty tricks. This is another kind of lie—blaming somebody else for what you did.

And what's the truth? Ben Carson was going home to Florida to get a change of clothes and rest, and then he was invited to the National Prayer Breakfast.

Ted Cruz's campaign website posted a picture of Rubio and Obama shaking hands, obviously agreeing on a trade pact. But the image had been photoshopped, the smiling faces of Rubio and Obama superimposed on another photograph. This carries layers of lies to it! It falls into the tabloid category, and it should be far beneath any candidate.

Ted Cruz spokesman Rick Tyler then reposted a video, originally from the *Daily Pennsylvanian* blog, of Marco Rubio walking past Cruz's father and a staffer who was reading the Bible. The video subtitled Rubio's barely audible words as "Not many answers in it." It is believed that what he really said was, "All the answers are in there." What a lie, what a defamation of character, and what an insult to the father and the staffer who obviously respected the Bible! Anyone who knows anything about Rubio would know that he is a church-goer and a conservative Evangelical, and he certainly would respect the Bible.

Lest anyone think these three dirty tricks were mistakes, Cruz added another one: Marco Rubio received an endorsement from Trey Gowdy, an Evangelical Christian. A post on a fake Facebook page shortly before the South Carolina primary had Gowdy saying he had changed his mind and now endorsed Cruz instead! Gowdy demanded that Cruz repudiate the post; Cruz denied that he or his campaign were responsible.

These dirty tricks are the kind that little boys play on each other and then get sent to the principal's office. It's not only a lie, it's bad manners, and he should be ashamed of himself. If it is true that his communications manager did all of this behind his back, then Cruz is not a good judge of character, he doesn't respond fast enough to fix a problem, and he's not worthy to be a president.

Misleading the Public

In order to make an informed decision, voters need to know as much as possible about a candidate. When I first started looking for campaign lies, my researcher said she couldn't find anything on Bernie Sanders. Shortly after that, however, Bernie Sanders ran several misleading statements: He ran banners on his mailings and e-mails implying that he had been endorsed by the AARP and by the League of

Conservation Voters. He also implied that he had been endorsed by the *Des Moines Register* newspaper, but they endorsed Clinton instead, and he well knew it. He quickly took these banners off of his mailings, once these misleading statements were exposed.

Embellishment: The Story That's Not Quite True

For any candidate, there's a benefit to having a good backstory. Voters want to hear stories about the candidate's parents and grandparents who have experienced dramatic events in their lives. Candidates want those events to fit the electorate they're trying to win over. Sometimes they embellish the story or make up parts of it. If they say it with great conviction, listeners believe it, because the candidates, of all people, should know their own past.

Trump likes to imply that he's a self-made man, although his father owned apartment buildings in Brooklyn and was quite well off. Marco Rubio tells us that his parents fled Cuba when Castro took over in 1959, but they actually came in 1956, in order to find better opportunities in the United States. The story of parents fleeing Castro, however, works much better with the Cuban Americans in Florida.

Ben Carson said he was offered a scholarship to West Point, although West Point knows nothing about that. He has told stories of his bravery and honesty, and he said he was featured in the Yale newspaper for his bravery, but no record of this article can be found.

Hillary Clinton says she was named after Sir Edmund

Hillary, but he didn't climb Mt. Everest until several years after she was born. For this embellishment, it's hard to know whether to blame her or her mother.

Sliding Around the Truth

There is a presumption that Hillary Clinton is not to be trusted. Of course, one can make the case that neither is Trump or Cruz or Rubio. But for some reason, aspersions seem to stick more to Hillary than to others. This may possibly be true because Bill Clinton's eight years in office were plagued by a number of attacks and accusations, although some were shown to be false. Clearly, there are times when Hillary has made a little slide around the truth. It is more difficult to uncover the lies about Hillary, because many presume she has lied about some things but those presumptions come, to a great extent, from conservatives who have high stakes in proving she's untrustworthy.

It seems to me that Hillary's law background has taught her to be very careful about the words that she chooses. As a result, sometimes she uses a word that people misunderstand but, of course, she can deny that she said what they thought she said. Her husband had exactly the same habit. Sometimes she is very careful about choosing the word that tells the truth, but her opponents mislead the public by claiming she said something that she really hadn't said. It is difficult to uncover all the truth about the Benghazi attack on September 11, 2012 and, after reading innumerable articles about it, I'm less clear than I was at the beginning. Of course, the Congressional committees aren't sure either, at this point. Her accusers say, among other things, that she blamed an anti-Muslim video for the attack rather than blaming Al Qaeda. This doesn't seem to be true. In the transcripts, she mentions that this anti-Muslim video led to thirty or forty protests against American embassies. However, the Ambassador's compound in Benghazi was not an embassy, and she only mentions this video as one of the reasons that might have given rise to the attack because one of the attackers mentioned the video. What Clinton's critics never talk about was her request for more security, which was denied by the Republican Congress. This exposed the Americans left in Benghazi to danger. On the other hand, although four people were killed, many others were saved by the fast action of the covert CIA security team.

Denial

Candidates deny facts and history. Most Republican candidates deny climate change, although most scientists are clear that this is a reality.

Candidates switch their positions and pretend they did not say something, even though videos prove they did. Trump insists he was against the invasion of Iraq, despite proof that he was asked in 2002 on a radio show, "Are you in favor of invading Iraq?" and he replied, "I guess so." There is evidence that he changed his mind by 2004, but he still denies that he approved of the invasion earlier.

Both Marco Rubio and Ted Cruz keep denying their former positions on immigration. It is one thing to say that a position has changed, which often happens over a period of time. But in this case, they both deny ever having supported a bill for immigration, although their stances were there in plain sight, having been recorded several years ago.

The Spin

The spin takes the facts, whether good or bad, and tries to convince us that black and white are really grey. We often respond to the spin with an "Oh, really?" response, or "You've got to be kidding!" Ted Cruz ranked third in the South Carolina primary, even though he expected to come in second. He told his audience that his was an extraordinary finish and that everything was going very well. The next day, he fired his communications manager, showing that things weren't going very well at all. Ted Cruz also continually says that he's the only candidate who can defeat Trump because he defeated him in some of the states, although at the time of writing this book, he's still hundreds of delegates behind the front-runner. Almost all candidates try to spin the facts to their own advantage.

Over-Promising

Many times politicians make big promises to get elected, and then soon after break their promises. They tell us what we want to hear. Bernie Sanders has promised free college for everyone. Trump has promised he'll build a wall and

make America great again. Rubio promised he would win
the Florida primary and unite the country. Cruz has promised he'll beat Trump!

It's a matter of integrity that people carry out their com-
mitments. If they don't believe they can fulfill their vow,
they shouldn't be making it in the first place.

Labeling, Name-Calling, and Mud-Slinging

We also bear false witness by labeling others untruthfully.
Democrats have often been told we're "un-American" and
"unpatriotic" for questioning various policies of the government. Christian Democrats have often been told they're
"un-Christian" to question Republicans or to question
policies that seem to impinge on the religious freedom of
others. Some American citizens are told they are "unsup-
portive of our troops" if they question a war.

Why is labeling deceptive? First of all, none of us fits
neatly into categories. Even to call any of us "conservative"
or "liberal" does not fully comprehend our stances on all
issues. Many people are conservative on some issues, liberal on others.

Second, labeling is an obstacle to honest debate. Bullying and tyrannizing those who don't agree with us gets us
nowhere. Ideas are dismissed because they come from the
"other party." We hear more pontificating than communication. There is more libeling than listening.

Name-calling is an excuse for not dealing respectfully
with another person. It puts the label of "rejected" on that
person, and allows the name-caller to turn his back on him

or her and decide the other person's opinion doesn't matter. It's un-Christian, because it rejects a person Beloved of God. It is undemocratic, because it's classist to believe that one person is far better than another.

Name-calling is not the same as critiquing another person's recommendation of how to resolve a problem. In the latter case we are asked to put the emphasis on the idea, not to demean the person. Sanders and Clinton have worked very hard to keep the focus on policy and not to attack each other. In fact, they declare that they like each other and have stood up for each other against attacks from others.

There has been a great deal of name-calling and mudslinging from the Republican candidates who are front-runners. Donald Trump, particularly, loves to label other people and has the ability to make a name stick. But nothing sticks to Donald. In that way, he's like Ronald Reagan, who was called the "Teflon President" because no matter what illegalities he did and what accusations were leveled against him, nothing seemed to stick. He would smile and say he couldn't remember. Everyone would smile and let it go, because he was so charming and he seemed to be honest. Trump is a "Teflon candidate." Nothing sticks to him, although his attacks on other candidates stick to *them* because he knows exactly how to get their goat. Whether or not his attacks are true, it doesn't seem to matter.

That is obviously a great talent of his. He calls Ted Cruz "nasty," "Lyin' Ted," and "wacko," Jeb Bush is "low energy," women are "dogs," Rubio is "Little Marco," Ben Carson is "pathological" (likened to child molesters), Mexicans are "rapists" and "killers," and he won't call John McCain a war hero because Trump likes "people that weren't captured."

Hiding the Truth

In order to make good policies, legislators need to know the truth about a person, a policy, or an event.

We are not good witnesses if we don't identify hypocrisy, deception, secrets, and lies when we see them. When it comes to politics, we need to be skeptical because political animals take strong stands and unwavering positions, whether they're true or not and whether the candidate claims to be a Christian or not.

Chapter Nine

Crossing the Political Divide

*"You should all agree among yourselves
and be sympathetic; love the brothers, have
compassion and be self-effacing. Never repay
one wrong with another, or one abusive word
with another, instead, repay with a blessing."*
1 Peter 3:8–9

We say we want Christian values in our government, but we won't get them by fighting with each other. Instead of wasting energy on the fight, why not focus on the solution? If Roman Christians and Greek Christians and Egyptian Christians could get along in the early years of the Christian era (although with a great deal of scolding from Paul as well as others), certainly we can begin to try to create a better nation, and a better world, together.

Jesus and Paul saw that judgment of each other, stemming from pride and self-righteousness, were major obstacles to advancing the Kingdom on Earth. A number of times, Paul explained that diversity was good. We all have different gifts. It is through these different gifts that we build up the Kingdom of God, not by all trying to be alike.[1]

Begin with Empathy and Compassion

In the 1980s, my husband and I were part of a workshop sponsored by the National Conference of Christians and Jews (NCCJ). The NCCJ was founded in the late 1920s by a Catholic priest, a Jewish rabbi, and a Protestant minister to help people understand where their prejudices came from and how to overcome them. By the 1990s, it had expanded to include other religions, races, and groups, so it changed its name to The National Conference for Community and Justice. The founders of the organization recognized that the first step in breaking stereotypes was simply bringing people together and having them begin talking to each other. Our group was made up of twelve participants—one-third Jewish, one-third Catholic, and one-third Protestant.

One of the Jewish women recounted how difficult Christmas was for her. She felt that Christianity was blaring at her, constantly, with little respect for her own religion. I had never looked at Christmas through the eyes of another religion, so this was a revelation to me. She cried as she talked about her pain created by my favorite season. I felt as if I had stepped across a religious divide into her viewpoint, and understood something about the isolation that she must be feeling.

Crossing the divide begins with empathy and compassion. We have to walk around in the other person's shoes for a bit. We have to be willing to admit that the other has a valid point of view. We have to care enough to be willing to accept, sympathize, and empathize with another person.

The workshop had a profound effect on me, because I learned that I could cross over. I wanted to do a similar workshop with Christians and Muslims, since I knew little about Islam and had nothing but stereotypes to guide me. I wondered what I'd learn by talking to Buddhists or Hindus. It never occurred to me, at that time, that Christianity would become so split that I would see the need for people of different denominations and different political parties to talk to each other and to break the stereotypes they have of each other.

Give Our Viewpoint

I used to be intimidated when I talked to conservatives, because I felt they would judge my theology as being far too liberal. I would become very quiet. Or I would tell them only those perceptions with which they would agree. As a result, I cowered before my brothers and sisters in Christ. In retrospect, I realized that I was keeping us from having an honest conversation. I resisted being truly present in the conversation. I didn't trust their kindness and acceptance. I presumed that all conservatives were judgmental, which wasn't true.

Perhaps more important, I was distrusting my own spirituality, even though I spent at least as much time attending church as they did, at least as much time reading the Bible as they did, and at least as much time studying theology as they did, and I had spent at least as much time as a Christian as they had. I decided it was time to speak the truth, but also be willing to listen to their viewpoint. I found this to be difficult because my viewpoint had been developed over a long period of time, and eliciting their responses is often presumed to come from unclarity about my own position. I was fairly clear about what I believed. I discovered that being open to another opinion did not mean I was unclear about my own.

Learning to share opinions with compassion in order to connect us with each other and to understand each other takes training and practice. The political and religious arenas seem to be an emotional minefield of vehement opinions that many refuse to enter for fear of destroying relationships that are kind and loving in all other areas.

Since the Bible teaches to "fear not," I realized that I had to speak the truth about political and social issues that mattered to me. I realized the importance of listening, discussing, and being vulnerable by clarifying areas where I was struggling, and trying to work together to find good and workable solutions.

I discovered that most conservatives aren't quite as closed and intolerant as I had thought. In fact, I have had many rich and wonderful and compassionate conversations with my conservative friends about homosexuality, abortion, and politics.

In the same way, I've talked to liberals whose lives were very much directed by their Christian faith and who had penetrating insights into the Bible and into how to practice their spirituality. I found that many liberals pray daily, have devotional time every day, and love the Limitless God.

With all Christians, I found we had many areas of agreement, if we could get past the rhetoric and the stereotyping, which were serving no one, especially not God.

Stop the Rhetoric!

We can't be effective until we get past the strife and see the larger picture. In many passages, the Bible sees dissension and strife as one of the biggest problems between Christians. Over and over again, the Bible tells us to love one another. Clearly the early Christians were much like our Congress and the many spokespersons for both the Republican and Democratic parties, judging and blaming and creating anything but a loving community. It is easy for us to want to be right, rather than to want to be effective. It is easy for us to over-identify with a party, because it gives us a strong sense of identity. But there is only one identity we need—followers of Christ.

Quakers believe that we find Unity by first listening to each other. When Hillary Clinton ran for senator, she had a "listening campaign." Many had no idea what to think of a candidate who focused on listening, not talking. They had never heard of such a thing. But she wanted to know what the voters thought, what they cared about. And she won with a good solid majority.

Without really listening, we presume what the other person wants and needs and means simply by their words. When we listen deeply to our neighbors, we hear the struggles and the striving for answers and the false starts and the figuring it out that are part of the process of intuiting what the Spirit is telling us.

Listening has always been difficult for me. From the moment I learned to talk, I loved to talk. I was a bit of a blabbermouth until I developed a friendship with a great listener, who taught me that listening was filled with surprises and was, at times, even more interesting than my own seemingly brilliant ideas. I still talk too much, but I'm working on it.

Find the Right Models for Discussion

There are some good models for how issues can be discussed, and sometimes even resolved.

Throughout our country's history, there have been town meetings to bring communities together to discuss issues. These can be healthy, provided that the meetings are open to every viewpoint, and are not stacked with people who will only say what the politician wants to hear. Potentially volatile discussions need a moderator to separate facts from opinion and judgment. This presidential election season has featured many town meetings, which allow the candidates to take a break from fighting each other. They're able to clarify their policies and open up to the audience without being on the defensive.

The town meetings and speeches of Democratic candidates have seen Bernie Sanders listening to a weeping woman describe the struggles of working three to five jobs at minimum wage yet being unable to buy Christmas gifts for her children.

Look For, and Affirm, Agreement

There is far more agreement than we might expect. Republicans and Democrats actually agree on the importance of many issues and have a desire to resolve them. Unfortunately, the government is so polarized that they won't work together. Over sixty percent of Republicans, Democrats, and Independents agree that we need to defend our country against terrorism, strengthen the economy, make Social Security sound, and reduce health care costs. Occasionally, Republicans and Democrats work together to create bills to resolve these problems.[2]

I don't expect that we would be able to talk to the vicious extremists who exist in every religion and every party. But it's not imperative that we do. If Christians in communities started talking to each other, and did not allow the extremists as our representatives, we could reach agreement in many areas of public policy. When we band together in areas of agreement, our effectiveness ripples outward, so that the power of the public voice of Christianity no longer comes from the extremists, but from a place of reason and civility.

When the voice of democracy comes from a more central and reasonable position, we have a more civil society that runs the way it was meant to run—with checks and balances, and without secrecy and power out of control.

It would seem that it would be impossible for diverse groups to reach consensus on any issue, particularly when there seems to be so little that we can agree on. But consensus, or near-consensus, is possible. The Quakers have been practicing it for more than 300 years and have been effective in using it for such social policies as eradicating slavery, reforming prisons, bringing about equal rights for the disenfranchised, and setting up programs to work for peace.

Many United Nations policies, particularly the position papers created from the organization's international conferences, are created through consensus. When I attended the 1995 UN Women's Conference in Beijing, China, I was surprised that it was possible to create a document through consensus that represented the views of women from many different cultural, ethnic, and religious backgrounds, as well as gays and straights, religious and not religious. There was much that we could agree on.

When there is consensus, or near-consensus, on issues, there is no one to sabotage the solution. Energy is not wasted on bickering. All work together, and the power of many voices creates effective legislation.

Certainly we cannot expect complete consensus in our government with the myriad of opinions on most issues. But there may be places where consensus or near-consensus can be reached. In the Democratic and Republican platforms of 2012 (at the time of writing, the 2016 platforms were still in the future), there seemed to be some agreement on reducing emissions from cars, eliminating discrimination (although the Republicans did not include gender orientation), creating new jobs, and strengthening the middle class. This should work as a good starting point for agreement.

However, on Inauguration Day in 2009, a group of Republicans met and made a decision to block Barrack Obama on anything he proposed, regardless of common ground in the past. This decision has brought our government to a halt, has created more partisanship in Congress, and has given Congress the lowest rating by citizens in the history of the United States. It has also created an ineffective Congress that has been bogged down by numerous votes to de-fund the Affordable Care Act, even though every vote is defeated and takes valuable time away from other issues. This kind of divisiveness is clearly not good for anybody.

Create Partnerships

There are those in Congress who are crossing the political divide. As a senator, Hillary Clinton was particularly effective at this. She co-sponsored a number of bills with Republicans. Some of these partnerships were surprising and unlikely. Senator Clinton partnered with former House Speaker Newt Gingrich to help pass a bill to increase electronic record-keeping in the health care industry. This helps to make the health care system more efficient and to reduce medical errors and sloppy records.

In fact, Gingrich, who once led the fight for impeaching Bill Clinton, has good things to say about Hillary Clinton: She's "very practical . . . very smart and very hard working . . . I have been very struck working with her."[3] He said that he had been impressed by the job she had done as senator, and that she had what it took to be the Democratic nominee for president. She's also worked on bills with Lindsey Graham, Tom DeLay, and John McCain—whom she openly says she truly likes and respects. Clinton believes that in order to get things done, people need to develop relationships and spend time together. Not all of this time needs to be political time but can be social time as well. When she was a senator, she belonged to a bipartisan women's group and a bipartisan prayer group.

Other senators have also worked together on bills that will make the government more effective, as well as helping citizens. Bipartisan bills to expand the accountability and openness of government were introduced by Senators John Cornyn (R-Texas) and Patrick Leahy (D-Vermont). George W. Bush and Ted Kennedy worked together to structure the "No Child Left Behind" bill. Bipartisan bills have been co-sponsored to combat human trafficking and slavery, and to overhaul the nation's immigration laws in order to provide a path to citizenship for millions of unauthorized immigrants.

For many laws, there is often an unlikely coalition of Democrats and Republicans bringing together business groups and labor unions, farm workers and growers, and occasionally pro-choice and pro-life proponents.

Jim Wallis, an evangelical liberal and author of the best-selling book *God's Politics,* has worked with Senator Rick Santorum as well as with Democrats on antipoverty proposals. Broad-based Christian groups have also backed efforts to combat AIDS, and have backed peacemaking groups sent to the Sudan.

Look for True Christian Dialogue

Quakers use the metaphor of the Light to emphasize the many Scriptural verses about turning toward the Light of Christ. The Light overcomes the darkness. We talk about seeking the Light, running toward the Light, trying to live in the Light. We can cross the political divide between Christians if we look for the Light and affirm wherever it is shining and whoever is carrying the Light. If we see Truth, then let us affirm it, whether it comes from conservatives or liberals, Republicans or Democrats. If we see partial truths, then let us affirm those as well. Even a sliver of Light can begin to pierce the darkness.

If we learn to discern the log in our own eye, and are willing to admit that we might be wrong, certainly that ability can lead us also to discerning where Truth and Light reside.

What Are We to Do as Christians?

There seem to be some consistent issues where the ideals of the Democratic Party and the ideals of Christianity come together. We are to:

- Help the poor, the needy, the widows and the orphans, the disadvantaged; those who are on the bottom rung of the ladder. Stand by them, and with them.
- Care for the oppressed, and be an advocate for those who have nowhere to turn.
- Be good and responsible stewards of this Garden, which we've been asked to care for; be visionaries in our policy in order to better care for the earth.
- Be inclusive and caring for others; love our enemies, and love our neighbors as ourselves.
- Be peacemakers, by forming coalitions; by being good friends with our allies; by practicing diplomacy. Be

strong and wise on issues of national defense, but also be creative in our methods. In the best of all worlds, we would beat our swords into plowshares, and study war no more.

- Judge rightly; be open to wisdom from wherever it may come; hope in the future; and always, continue to love our neighbor against all odds.

Christians, whether Republicans or Democrats, could do much to cross the political divide by asking their leaders to tone down the rhetoric and by reaching to span the chasm that seems to separate us. That might mean asking their powerhouse spokespersons to show a little more love in their statements. It might mean asking members of Congress to show more respect for their fellow Christians.

I would ask the same of the Democrats—that they censor each other when necessary, reach across the divide to try to form partnerships, and not assume that there is no common ground.

I would ask my Republican and Democratic friends to not look for the bad in each other, applauding when they find it, but to affirm that which is good, valuable, helpful, and effective—wherever it may come from.

I would ask the media to stop buying into this divisiveness because they think it makes good news. They are not serving the truth if they show only one side of the issue. I am not suggesting that they stop airing the views of conservative Christians. But they need to recognize, publicly, that there are hundreds of other Christians who can balance the views of all the conservative and fundamentalist commentators.

Perhaps we need to rethink our overall goal. Is it to win elections? To be the party that is always right? To denounce the others, and let the country know how wrong those people are? Or is it to create policy with values that promote the Good? I expect we can agree on at least some of this policy.

Of non-Christians, I would ask that you not judge us by the loudest and most dramatic of our members. Forgive us for the times we have treated you badly. Read the Gospels to find out who this person named Jesus truly was. And know that at least some of us recognize that your highest values, and our highest values, are not just Christian values, but universal values that can bring us together as we try to create a just and compassionate society.

All of us must seek light and love and truth. When we see it, we must look to it and serve it.

Study Guide

This study guide is intended to provide an opportunity for you to reflect on your faith, either by yourself or in a group. You might pick and choose certain chapters, depending on what is currently in the news or of particular interest to your group. You may want more than one session on each issue. I doubt if you can cover the "War and Peace" chapter in an hour or two. In some of the questions below, I mention other resources that you might want to pursue; you also may want to study some of the books mentioned in the chapter endnotes, which follow this study guide.

It is my hope that Democrats and Republicans can study these issues together, examine issues in the light of Scripture, and perhaps even be moved to action. You may be led, as a group, to write a letter to the editor of your local newspaper, or respond in some other ways. I would recommend that you look for consensus if you are doing this as a group.

The study guide can be used by Christian or secular groups. The questions under (**A**) are more general nonreligious questions. The (**B**) questions are designed to lead to reflection and discussion and, hopefully, help deepen one's spiritual response.

Those who aren't Christian may want to study some of

these issues from the viewpoint of their own spiritual tradition and possibly refer to that tradition's own religious and spiritual writings.

Chapter One
How Would Jesus Vote?

1. **(A)** Look at the various definitions of "conservative" and "liberal." In what ways do you see yourself as conservative? In what ways are you a liberal? What are the dangers of both points of view when taken to the extreme?

   (B) Read Matthew 7:1–2, I Corinthians 5:12–13, Luke 12:14, and John 12:47. Why do you think Jesus and Paul so often asked the early Christians to "Judge not, that you be not judged"? What are the problems and consequences that result from a judgmental attitude?

2. **(A)** If you're a Republican, what are the policies within your own party that you feel are ill-advised or problematical? What policies or people within the Democratic Party do you most admire? If you're a Democrat, what policies in your own party bother you? What Republican policies and people do you admire? Why? (If you can't find any, you may be demonizing the other side and need a more open mind. Think harder!)

   (B) Look at the values that are implied in Jesus' actions in I Corinthians 7, John 8, and Matthew 5 and 18. How did Jesus change the law? Why did he change it?

Chapter Two
The Poor, the Needy, Widows, and Orphans

1. **(A)** Which values that help the poor and disadvantaged would you like to see exhibited in your country? Which of these values need help from the state? What can best be done by individuals or groups?

   (B) What is your church's stand on caring for the poor and needy? Print out a copy of your church's doctrine (most are found on the Internet) and discuss its stand. Do you agree, or disagree, with most, or all, aspects of the doctrine? Who does your church help in their priority of needs? Church members? New attenders? The neighborhood? The community? People from other religions or other cultures who are in need? How well does your church do?

2. **(A)** Why are there poor people? To what extent is it their own fault? What social and political structures contribute to poverty? How much interaction have you personally had with the poor? Were any stereotypes broken as a result of being close to poverty or to those who are poor?

   (B) Read the Bible verses on caring for the poor that are mentioned in the beginning of this chapter. Why do you think God cares so much for the poor? To what extent do you have problems with the poor? Are you afraid of them? Feel burdened by them? Feel vulnerable because they might want what you have and steal from you? Why does God call them "blessed"?

3. **(A)** What government programs do you know about, or would like to see, that would create a more compassionate society?

(B) Print out a copy of the "Call to Civic Responsibility" from the National Evangelical Association (on the Web at *www.nae.net/images/civic_responsibility.pdf*). Read the sections that have to do with caring for the poor and needy. Notice that no legislation is mentioned. What government programs do you know about, or would like to see, that would address these issues? What church or charity programs could help? Keep in mind that the poor and needy may not be Christians. How would that change your understanding of your responsibility?

Chapter Three
Beautiful Savior, King of Creation

1. **(A)** What in nature do you love? The sea? The forests? The mountains? The birds and animals? How do they nourish you? To what extent do they enrich your life? How often do you spend time allowing nature to have an effect on your life?

(B) Read Genesis 1. Why did God call the creation "Good"? What's good about it? How does this Goodness impact your own personal life? To what extent do you appreciate and love God's creation? To what extent do you find God present in creation?

2. **(A)** Create a short paragraph about your philosophy on nature. What are some bills or policies you would like to see the government support to better preserve the earth?

(B) Read your church's doctrine on the environment. If your church doesn't have one, read the Quaker doctrine or Church of the Brethren doctrine. You can find some of these at *www.webofcreation.org* and at *www.brethren.org/ac/ac_statements/91Creation.htm#11.*
Do you see a relationship between your religion and the environment? What more could you, charities, and the government do to protect this legacy?

Chapter Four
The Ethical Dilemma of Abortion

1. **(A)** What are your views about abortion? How have you arrived at these views? Have there been experiences, readings, discussions, and so on, that have led you to your personal philosophy?

(B) Whether you're pro-choice or pro-life, which Bible verses or theology support your viewpoint? Which verses or theology can you think of to support the opposite view? Why do you think this is such a difficult ethical problem?

2. **(A)** What can be done to stop unwanted pregnancies? Are you aware of programs (whether from government,

charities, the church, etc.) that are effective? Are there other possibilities that you can think of?

(B) What is a Christian's responsibility to help unwanted children? What are you willing to do? What is your church willing to do?

3. (A) Read the Democrats for Life policy statement found at *www.democratsforlife.org.*

Compare this to the Republican stance about abstinence. Do you find elements in both are helpful? Or unhelpful?

(B) Compare the theological statements from *www.consistentlife.com* and the Focus on the Family document found at *www.focusonyourchild.com/hottopics/a00001286.cfm.* To what extent do you find these arguments compelling? Are there loopholes?

Chapter Five
Homosexuals: Civil Rights, Same-Sex Marriage

1. (A) If you're heterosexual, what is your experience with homosexuals? Do you have gay friends, associates, or acquaintances? How much have you learned about homosexuality from them? How much from the media?

In what ways have you experienced differences between yourself and homosexuals? If your group includes homosexuals, discuss how they experience differences between themselves and heterosexuals. Move beyond defining people purely in terms of their sexuality.

If you have not known homosexuals as friends or neighbors, or as members of your congregation, your group might ask someone to come to talk about their lives. You can contact a local Gay and Lesbian Alliance, or contact a Metropolitan Community Church, whose ministry is centered on gays and lesbians.

(B) How do you feel about gay marriages? C. S. Lewis says that maybe marriage should be a sacred ceremony, not a civil union, so that churches decide who they'll marry, and everyone else can marry through a judge. Is this a good idea? What about gays who aren't religious but still want to be married? What about heterosexuals who want some kind of religious ceremony, even though they are only nominally religious? Do you think society will be harmed, or not, by gay marriages?

2. **(A)** Consider some equal rights that homosexuals want, such as no discrimination in jobs or housing, and being able to adopt as a single person, in much the same way that a heterosexual single person is able to adopt. Then consider some of the benefits that gay couples in long-term relationships want—hospital visiting rights, the right to inherit, the right to the other person's Social Security benefits upon their death in long-term gay relationships, the right to have and raise children, and so on.

Which of these rights do you think are fair? Which are not? Why?

(B) Read Genesis 19, Leviticus 18 and 20, I Timothy, Romans 1, I Corinthians 6, I Timothy 1–10. Discuss the interpretations of these verses (as found within Chapter Five). You may also want to read Focus on the Family's comments, which can be found at *www.family.org/ married/topics/a0025114.cfm*

What are the problems in interpreting these passages? Where are they clear and not clear?

What other degrading sexual behavior might you add to these lists? How does sex use people? How does it harm people? Why does the Bible value sex in a mutual and loving relationship, but speak so harshly about these other forms of sex?

3. (A) If you're a heterosexual, put yourself in the place of a homosexual in American society. What problems would you face? How would you feel about yourself? How would you internalize social and political attitudes? If you're gay, put yourself in the place of a heterosexual. Why do you think they have a problem with homosexuals?

(B) What do you think should be done about homosexuals in American society? What would you consider just? Fair? Caring? Loving? Christian?

Chapter Six
War and Peace

1. (A) Are you a pacifist, or have you known pacifists? On what philosophy or theology do pacifists base their

stand? What do you see as the pluses and minuses of that philosophy?

(B) Why do you think the early Christians were told not to take part in war? What changed? Why did it change? What would happen if Christians continued to take this nonviolent stand?

2. **(A)** Discuss the Just War theory in relationship to several wars. Did the wars fulfill all the criteria? Are the criteria realistic and practical, or useless and impractical?

(B) What is the occasion for war? What can we do, as Christians, to take away the problems that lead to war? What can individuals, churches, and a government that is led by Christian principles do to help take away the occasion for war?

Chapter Seven
Confronting Terrorism and Fear

1. **(A)** What problems in our country cause you to fear? Discuss the ways that fear begins and is maintained.

(B) What were the fearful situations in the Hebrew Scriptures that the Israelites encountered? Were they resolved? If so, how? What were the situations in Jesus' time, and shortly after, that caused fear? How did the early Christians deal with them? Were these methods effective?

2. **(A)** Brainstorm actions and policies that our nation could take to confront the problems of terrorism. Is it possible to be as wise as serpents but as innocent as doves when confronting these?

(B) If you are in a situation of tension, conflict, and fear, in what ways do you draw on your faith and your relationship with God? How has your response changed the dynamic of the situation? Has it been effective? What can you take from this situation that would be helpful for our international relationships?

Chapter Eight
Secrets, Lies, and Deceptions

1. **(A)** What is the difference between a secret and a lie? What are valid secrets? When are secrets not valid but used to cover up? List some of the secrets and cover-ups that you've observed in our American history.

(B) When Jesus said, "The Truth will make you free" (John 8:32), what did he mean? How is truth freeing?

2. **(A)** Why do politicians feel the need to lie? Is a lie ever justified?

(B) In the 1960s, Joseph Fletcher wrote a book called *Situation Ethics*, in which he argues that Jesus followed situation ethics when he picked corn on the Sabbath, let the adulterous woman go rather than have her stoned, and healed on the Sabbath, among other examples. As a Christian, to what extent are we to hold to a single standard of truth, and to what extent do we need to recognize the moral and ethical complexities of certain situations? Is there a governing principle that we can follow, such as "do no harm" or "whatever the Bible says" or "never lie" or . . . ???

Chapter Nine
Crossing the Political Divide

1. (A) How difficult is it for you to cross the political divide? How difficult is it to talk to someone from the other party? Why do you think this problem is so prevalent?

   (B) Some people of one party hate those from the other party. What are the qualities that you could admire in those from the other party if you could put your conflict, or even hatred, aside? If you can't find any good qualities, read or ask others; you may have objectified the Other, which rejects that person as the Beloved of God.

2. (A) Where do you see places of agreement between the two parties? On what issues, if they could be seen in a broad perspective, might we find agreement? Consider the issues mentioned in this book—ranging from ecology and health care to the national debt, war, terrorism, homosexuality, abortion, and so on.

(B) What could you do to help create less divisiveness and more unity among Christians? What could your church, or any religious or charitable group you belong to, do? Might you create discussion groups? Or a reading list? A prayer group? Would the example of Kelly Williams work in your group? Are there other models you could use?

Notes

Introduction

1. One only has to read the newspapers or go to a bookstore to see the number of books by Republicans that attack Democrats. For instance, in his book *Let Freedom Ring: Winning the War of Liberty over Liberalism*, conservative television commentator Sean Hannity says that if the Left takes power, civilization is at stake. In his book *Deliver Us from Evil*, he lists "evil" people, parties, and groups, including Bill and Hillary Clinton, Jimmy Carter, the Democratic Party, John Kerry, Al Gore, Edward M. Kennedy, John Edwards, Joseph Lieberman, Richard Gephardt, Howard Dean, Wesley Clark, and the United Nations. He blames Bill Clinton for the September 11 attacks. These ideas can also be found in a number of articles including "Democrats Sensitive to Alleged 'Assault on People of Faith'" by Susan Jones, CNSNews.com (*Morning Editor*, April 19, 2005); "Bill Frist's Christian Jihad," from watchdog.com, April 16, 2005; Colbert I. King, "Hijacking Christianity," *Washington Post*, April 23, 2005; and Leo Sandon, "Who Are

These People of Faith," *Tallahassee Democrat*, April 30, 2005.

Chapter One
How Would Jesus Vote?

1. In 2004, 22 percent of Evangelicals voted for Kerry, 78 percent for Bush. More Latino Protestants (63 percent) voted for Bush, and more black Protestants (83 percent) voted for Kerry. About 77 percent of people of other faiths and 73 percent of Jews voted for Kerry. Pew Research, "Beyond Red vs. Blue," the 2005 Political Typology. See also "How the Faithful Voted: 2012 Preliminary Analysis," by Pew Research Centers, Religion and Public Life Project, November 27, 2012.
2. Galatians 5:22–23.
3. Matthew 25:35–37.
4. Galatians 5:19–21.
5. Matthew 15:11.
6. Genesis 4:7.
7. Jack Jenkins, "The Real Reason Trump Is Winning Evangelical Support: They're Just Not That 'Religious,'" *ThinkProgress.org*, January 27, 2016, at *http://thinkprogress.org/politics/2016/01/27/3743383/evangelicals-trump-are-not-religious/*.
8. Russell D. Moore, "Donald Trump Is Not the Moral Leader We Need," *National Review*, January 22, 2016, at *http://www.nationalreview.com/article/430119/donald-trump-russell-moore-not-moral-leader*.
9. Galatians 5:22–23.

10. Quoted from Juan Mateos in *God or Nations*, by William Durland (Baltimore: Fortkamp Publishing Company, 1989), pp. 53–55.

11. Deuteronomy 6:5, Mark 12:30.

12. Mary Dyer was one of the many Quakers who continually spoke out for religious freedom in Massachusetts, eventually being put to death for her beliefs. Her advocacy of religious freedom eventually led to religious freedom being included in our Constitution. Other sources about Quaker persecutions include "The Quakers: Hostile Bonnets and Gowns: Governor Endicott's Threat," *The Colonial Gazette*, 1998, 1999, 2000, *www.mayflowerfamilies.com/enquirer/quakers. htm*, retrieved October 12, 2005; and "Quaker History," from Wikipedia, found at *http://en.wikipedia.org/wiki/ Quaker_history*, retrieved October 12, 2005.

13. Max Savelle, "Roger Williams, a Minority of One," in *The American Story: The Age of Exploration to the Age of the Atom* (Great Neck, NY: Channel Press, 1956), pp. 52–53.

14. Herbert J. Storing, *What the Anti-Federalists Were For: The Political Thought of the Opponents of the Constitution* (Chicago: University of Chicago Press, 1981), p. 47.

15. Thomas Jefferson, *Notes on the State of Virginia*, 1781.

16. Thomas Jefferson, Letter to the Danbury Connecticut Baptist Association, January 1, 1802.

17. T. Harry Williams, "Abraham Lincoln: Pragmatic Democrat," in *The Enduring Lincoln*, ed. Norman Graebner (Urbana, IL: University of Illinois Press, 1959), p. 34.

18. This is discussed in several articles including: Bob Moser, "The Crusaders: Christian Evangelicals Are

Plotting to Remake America in Their Own Image,"
Rolling Stone, April 7, 2005; Stanley Kurtz, "Dominionist Domination," *National Review,* July 24, 2005;
"Christian Dominionists stand against liberalism"
From Web-Ministry, *www.web-ministry.com/linaer/
php?postID=8632,* January 26, 2005, retrieved June,
2005; Peter Wallsten, "The Nation: 2 Evangelicals Want
to Strip Courts' Funds; Taped at a private conference,
the leaders outline ways to punish jurists they oppose"
[Home Edition] *Los Angeles Times,* April 22, 2005;
Daniel Berke, "Five Facts About Dominionism," Religion News Service, first posted 9/1/2011; "Christian Dominionists in the US Congress Today: A Review of the
Book, Christian Nation," *Theocracy Watch;* and "God
and Government: Christian Dominionists of the GOP,"
The News Observer.

19. Chris Hedges, "Soldiers of Christ II: Feeling the Hate
with the National Religious Broadcasters," p. 6. Article
posted on Harpers.org on May 30, 2005.

20. "Religious affiliation of U.S. Congress: 109th U.S. Congress (2005–2006)." From Web page *www.adherents.
com/adh_congress.html,* retrieved on July 15, 2005.

21. C. S. Lewis, "Equality," from *Present Concern: Essays by
C. S. Lewis* in *The Quotable Lewis,* ed. Walter Hooper
(San Diego: Harcourt Brace Jovanovich, 1986), p. 17.

22. Among other verses are Matthew 6:24, 25:15–30; Luke
3:14, 16; John 2:14–17; I Timothy 6:10; Hebrews 13:5; Matthew 25:15–30; Luke 15.

23. "Biggest Deficit in History? Yes and No," FactCheck.org,
February 27, 2004. *www.factcheck.org/article148.html*
and Terence Samuel, "$7,782,816,546,352 In Debt," from
The American Prospect. Reported on CBSNews.com,

Washington, August 12, 2005. See also "Republican Debt," from *http://zfacts.com/book/export/html/260*, January 11, 2012, and "History of the United States Public Debt," from Wikipedia.

24. Jenice Robinson, "Candidates' Tax Cuts Unequivocally Skew Toward the Wealthy," *taxjusticeblog.org*, November 10, 2015; Eric Reed Follow, "Which Republican Candidate Will Lower Your Tax Bill the Most?" *thestreet. com*, January 24, 2016; and Kate Drew, "This is What Trump's Border Wall Could Cost US," special to *CNBC. com*, October 9, 2015.

25. Zach Carter, "Everything You Need to Know About the Republican Candidates' Tax Plans," *huffingtonpost. com*, November 10, 2015.

26. John 4.

27. Luke 10:38–42.

28. Luke 8:1–3.

29. Luke 10:29–37.

30. Matthew 21:31.

31. Luke 23:43.

32. I Corinthians 7.

33. John 8.

34. Matthew 18:22.

35. Leviticus 19:18.

36. Romans 12:19–21.

37. Matthew 5:21–26.

38. Matthew 5:43–44; Luke 6:27, 10:27; Romans 12:19–20.

39. Matthew 5:42.

40. Matthew 12:1, 10; Luke 6:1, 7.

41. "William Penn, Founder of Colonies," in "The American Story" Papers 1959, by Carl Bridenbaugh, p. 48.

42. Durland, "William Penn, James Madison, and the His-

torical Crisis in American Federalism," by William Durland, *Studies in American History*, Volume 28 (Lewiston, NY: The Edwin Mellen Press, 2000), p. 21.

43. Ibid., p. 20.
44. Ibid., p. 13.
45. Ibid., p. 22.

Chapter Two
The Poor, the Needy, Widows, and Orphans

1. Isaiah 10: 1–2 .
2. Psalm 72.
3. Psalms 49:13.
4. Amos 2.
5. Psalms 9–10, 34; Job 5; Psalms 107, 132; Jeremiah 2; Isaiah 25.
6. Leviticus 19; Deuteronomy 24; the Book of Ruth; Deuteronomy 14, 26; Leviticus 25, 14; Exodus 23.
7. Karl Barth, *Church Dogmatics IV, 3, The Doctrine of Reconciliation*, 2nd ed., trans. G.W. Bromiley (Edinburgh, Scotland: T & T Clark Ltd, 1958), p. 891.
8. Jeremiah 2:7.
9. Jeremiah 2:34.
10. Jeremiah 5:27–30.
11. Jeremiah 7:5–6.
12. Jeremiah 22:16–17.
13. Exodus 23:9.
14. Leviticus 19:33–34.
15. Emma Lazarus, "The New Colossus," 1883.
16. Deuteronomy 27:19.

17. Traditional Celtic "Rune of Hospitality," collected and translated by Kenneth MacLeod. Found in, for instance, Kieran J. O'Mahony, OSA, *What the Bible Says About the Stranger: Biblical Perspectives on Racism, Migration, Asylum, and Cross-Community Issues*, The Irish Inter-church Meeting, p. 2.

18. Matthew 6:33.

19. National Association of Evangelicals, "For the Health of the Nation: An Evangelical Call to Civic Responsibility." Paper presented and approved at The National Association of Evangelicals Conference, Spring, 2005.

20. From the Republican Platform 2012.

21. From a video shown on *Hardball with Chris Matthews* on MSNBC, April 30, 2014.

22. Gustavo Gutiérrez, *A Theology of Liberation: History, Politics, and Salvation*, rev. ed., trans. and ed. by Sister Caridad Inda and John Eagleson (Maryknoll, NY: Orbis Books, 1971, 1998), p. 9.

23. Ibid., p. 23.

24. Ibid., p. 35.

25. David Cay Johnston, "Richest Are Leaving Even the Rich Far Behind: Tax Laws Help to Widen Gap at Very Top," *New York Times*, June 5, 2005. Based on material collected from the Heritage Foundation, the Cato Institute, and Citizens for Tax Justice, as well as data from economists, the Federal Reserve's Consumer Finance Survey, the Tax Policy Center, the Urban Institute, the Brookings Institution, the IRS, and the President's 2006 budget.

26. Ted Turner, "Super-rich Don't Need Another Break," *USA Today*, March 12, 2001.

27. Luke 12:34.
28. John Johnson, "Five Mainline Protestant Leaders Call Bush's 2006 Budget 'unjust,'" from Worldwide Faith news archives, March 8, 2005.
29. Karl Barth, *The Epistle to the Romans*, trans. from 6th edition by Edwyn C. Hoskyns (London: Oxford University Press, 1933), p. 442.

Chapter Three
Beautiful Savior, King of Creation

1. There are many passages; among them are Genesis 1, Psalms 89:12, 148:5; Job 12:10, 14:15; Proverbs 8; John 1; Colossians 1:23; Revelation 4:11.
2. Genesis 1:28.
3. Bennett J. Sims, *Servanthood: Leadership for the Third Millennium* (Cambridge, MA: Cowley Publications, 1997), p. 147.
4. Numbers 32:22, 29; Jeremiah 34:11, 16; Esther 7:8; Nehemiah 5:5. Also Theodore Hiebert, "Rethinking Dominion Theology," *Direction*, Fall 1996, p. 19.
5. Sims, *Servanthood*, pp. 147–149. Also Hiebert, "Rethinking Dominion Theology," p. 18.
6. Brueggemann, Walter, "King in the Kingdom of Things" from *The Christian Century*, September 10, 1969, p. 1166.
7. Sims, *Servanthood*, p. 149.
8. David Tobin Asselin, "The Notion of Dominion in Genesis 1–3," *The Catholic Biblical Quarterly*, Vol. 16, p. 290.
9. Hiebert, "Rethinking Dominion Theology," p. 22. A similar interpretation is also given by Dr. Phyllis Trib-

ble, who taught a class I took at Immaculate Heart College Center. She talked a great deal about this word, *adamah*.

10. Genesis 2:15, 3:23.
11. Genesis 12:16, Exodus 4:23.
12. Hiebert, "Rethinking Dominion Theology," p. 23.
13. Ibid.
14. Ibid., p. 24.
15. Ibid.
16. Richard L. Means, from *Saturday Review*, December 2, 1967, quoted in "King in the Kingdom of Things" by Walter Brueggemann, from *The Christian Century*, Sept. 10, 1969, p. 1165. These ideas are also expressed in Mark 10:42–44 and I Peter 5:2–3.
17. Genesis 6, 7.
18. Proverbs 12:10.
19. Deuteronomy 22:4.
20. Deuteronomy 22:10.
21. Deuteronomy 20:19–20.
22. This theology has been written about by Matthew Fox, from *Original Blessings: A Primer in Creation Spirituality*, Jeremy P. Tarcher (New York: Putnam, 2000), p. 88. Originally published by Bear & Co., Inc., Santa Fe, New Mexico, 1983.
23. Ibid., pp. 89–90.
24. Pierre Teilhard de Chardin, *Hymn of the Universe* (New York: Harper Torchbooks, 1961), p. 124.
25. Fox, 119.
26. Terry L. Anderson and Clay J. Landry, "Exporting Water to the World." Published by Universities Council on Water Resources, USA Issue #118, January 2001.

27. Lester Brown, "'Plan B': The Rescue of a Planet and a Civilization," *Friends Journal*, October 2004.

28. Al Gore, *Earth in the Balance: Ecology and the Human Spirit* (New York: Plume Books, 1993) 264.

29. Ibid.

30. Ibid., p. 71.

31. Ibid., p. 73.

32. Ibid., p. 257.

33. Ibid., p. 262.

34. *The Ronan Farrow Daily Show*, MSNBC, April 25, 2014.

35. Democratic National Platform 2012.

36. Christine Todd Whitman, *It's My Party Too: The Battle for the Heart of the GOP and the Future of America* (New York: Penguin Press, 2005), p. 153.

37. Hillary Clinton, November 29, 2015. Quoted on her website, *hillaryclinton.com/issues/climate/*.

38. Woods Hole Oceanographic Institution, "Abrupt Climate Change: Bigger Hurricanes: A Consequence of Climate Change?" by Ruth Gorski Curry, September 20, 2004, from Ocean and Climate Change Institution. Also see "Simulated Increase of Hurricane Intensities in a CO_2–Warmed Climate" by Thomas R. Knutson, Robert E. Tuleya, Yhoshio Kurihara from *Science*, Vol. 279, February 13, 1998; "Warming world blamed for more strong hurricanes" by Fred Pearce from NewScientist.com, September 15, 2005; also see the *Time* magazine cover story from October 3, 2005, "Are We Making Hurricanes Worse?" as well as "Global Warming: The Culprit? Evidence mounts that human activity is helping fuel these monster hurricanes" by Jeffery Kluger, *Time*, October 3, 2005.

39. Jarrett Murphy, "Storm Front: In Global Warming's Kitchen, Hurricanes Love the Heat," *Village Voice*, September 27, 2005. The connection between hurricanes and global warming can be found in innumerable scientific articles, including several issues of *Science* magazine (Issues #279, #299) and *New Scientist* (June 25, 2005; September 15, 2005). See also Yereth Rosen, "Arctic Oil Search Moves to New Turf, New Controversies," *Christian Science Monitor*, May 16, 2005. Also quoted in David Remnick, "The White House Under Water," *The New Yorker*, September 12, 2005, pp. 36–37.

40. From the *New York Times* article, "Is This the End?" by James Atlas, November 24, 2013.

41. From the Democratic Party Platform, 2004.

Chapter Four
The Ethical Dilemma of Abortion

1. Matthew 5:32; also found in Luke 16:18 and Mark 10:11.

2. Psalm 100:3.

3. Isaiah 44:24; Job 31:15, 10:8–12; Psalm 139:13–16.

4. Isaiah 49:1, Jeremiah 1:5.

5. Exodus 4:11, Isaiah 45:9–11, Romans 9:20, Exodus 4:11, Isaiah 45:9–11, Romans 9:20. See also I Corinthians 6:19–20, Psalm 127:3, Ezekiel 18:4.

6. Steven D. Levitt and Stephen J. Dubner, *Freakonomics: A Rogue Economist Explores the Hidden Side of Everything* (New York: William Morrow, 2005), p. 118.

7. Ibid., p. 137.

8. Ibid., pp. 137–138.

9. Ibid., p. 137.

10. Ibid., p. 144.

11. Ibid., p. 141.

12. Keith Breckhouse, *Liberal America: Saving the USA Since 1776*, February 3, 2014, quoted from A Guttmacher Institute Study, *www.liberalamerica.org*.

13. Remarks by Senator Hillary Rodham Clinton to the NYS Family Planning Providers, January 24, 2005 in Albany, New York. lso Steven Ertelt, "Pro-life Group Seeks Meeting with Hillary Clinton to Discuss Abortion," LifeNews.com, February 9, 2005; and Andrew Sullivan, "TRB from Washington: Life Lesson," *The New Republic Online*, January 27, 2005.

14. "Plan to Reduce the Number of Abortions," Press Release, April 21, 2005. From Democrats for Life, found at *www.democratsforlife.org/Press/95-10%20release.html*. See also Susan Page, "The Changing Politics of Abortion," *USA Today*, May 1, 2005.

15. Quote from Congressman Tim Roemer at the Democrats for Life of America Press Conference, which introduced the 95-10 Initiative that would try to reduce 95% of abortions within 10 years, April 21, 2005.

Chapter Five
Homosexuals: Civil Rights, Same-Sex Marriage

1. Focus on the Family says it's about 2–3%; the Pikes Peak Gay and Lesbian Community Center uses 10%, including gays, lesbians, bisexual, and transgender.

2. Isaiah 45:9–13.

3. Romans 9:20.

4. Focus on the Family, "Responding to Pro-Gay Theology, What Does the Bible Really Say?" p. 11.

5. Peter J. Gomes, *The Good Book: Reading the Bible with Mind and Heart*, (San Francisco: Harper San Francisco, 1996), p. 171 . Originally published by William Morrow in hardcover, 1996.

6. Gen. 19:6–8.

7. Gray Temple, *Gay Unions: In the Light of Scripture, Tradition, and Reason* (New York: Church Publishing, 2004), p. 58.

8. Matthew 10:14–15, Luke 10:10–12.

9. Leviticus 20:9.

10. Leviticus 20:2.

11. Leviticus 20:10.

12. Leviticus 20:15.

13. Gomes, *The Good Book*, p. 153.

14. Ibid., p. 154.

15. From an e-mail exchange with Professor Gary A. Rendsburg, Rutgers University.

16. Temple, *Gay Unions*, pp. 52–53.

17. I Samuel 18:1.

18. I Samuel 18:3.

19. I Samuel 18:4.

20. I Samuel 20:3, 41.

21. II Samuel 1:26.

22. I Timothy 1:9–10.

23. Catherine Griffith, "The Bible and Same-Sex Relationship," *Friends Journal at 50: Quaker Thought and Life*

Today, January 2005, p. 14. Catherine Griffith was a pastor at Valley Mills (Indiana) Meeting; she holds a Ph.D. in Religious Ethics from the University of Virginia. Also see Gomes, *The Good Book*, p. 159.

24. Ibid.
25. Temple, *Gay Unions*, p. 77.
26. Ibid., p. 78.
27. Ibid., pp. 64–65.
28. Ibid., p. 70.
29. Ibid., pp. 71–72.
30. Ibid., pp. 72–73.
31. Romans 2:1–4.
32. James 4:12.
33. Gomes, *The Good Book*, p. 158.
34. Temple, *Gay Unions*, p. 74.
35. Temple, *Gay Unions*, p. 111.
36. Lewis, *Mere Christianity*, p. 102.

Chapter Six
War and Peace

1. William Durland, *God or Nations: Radical Theology for the Religious Peace Movement* (Baltimore: Fortkamp Publishing Company, 1989), p. 95.
2. Ibid., p. 95.
3. Isaiah 2:4, Hosea 2:18, Micah 4:30.
4. Revelation 21:4.
5. From Durango Friends Meeting (Colorado), "A Call for Justice, Not Revenge," submitted by co-clerks Ross

A. Worley and Kathryn Bowers, from Web site *http:// members.aol.com/friendsbul/peacemakers.html*, August 1, 2005.

6. From an interview with Col. Paul E. Pirog, Department Head, Department of Law, U.S. Air Force Academy. Col. Pirog, JAG officer, talked about this in a panel discussion, "The Iraq War and Conscientious Objection," at Colorado College, Colorado Springs, Colorado, March 31, 2005. The panel discussion was set up by the Justice and Peace Commission of Colorado Springs.

7. Robert A. Seeley, *Choosing Peace: a Handbook on War, Peace, and Your Conscience* (Philadelphia: Central Committee for Conscientious Objectors, 1994), p. 34.

8. From an interview with Dr. Norman Graebner, June 2005.

9. Seeley, *Choosing Peace*, p. 34.

10. Ibid.

11. Ibid.

12. Ibid.

13. Ibid.

14. From the Catechism of the Catholic Church.

15. Garry Wills, *Lincoln at Gettysburg: The Words that Remade America* (New York: Simon & Schuster, 1992), p. 179.

16. Ibid., p. 181.

17. From an interview with William Flavin, June 2005.

18. Seeley, *Choosing Peace*, p. 35.

19. 1970 Church of the Brethren, *Statement on War*.

20. Yaacov Bar-Siman-Tov, "Just Peace: Linking Justice to Peace," from a JAD-PbP Working Paper Series No.5, October 2009, p. 6.

21. Ibid., p. 14.

22. Ibid., p. 15.

23. Thom Shanker and Joel Brinkley, "U.S. Is Set to Sell Jets to Pakistan; India Is Critical," *New York Times*, March 26, 2005.

24. There are many studies of this, including Paul Bedard, "Price of Iraq, Afghan Wars Hits a Staggering $6 Trillion," *Washington Examiner*, March 2, 2015.

25. Kevin Baron, "For the U.S., War Against Qaddafi Cost Relatively Little: $1.1 Billion," in *The Atlantic*, 2014.

26. From a panel on the subject *Reality, Legality, & Morality of Drone Warfare*, held April 14, 2014, at The Colorado College, Colorado Springs. Panelists included Col. James L. Cook, head of the philosophy department at the U.S. Air Force Academy; Claude D'Estree, Director of International Human Rights Degree Program, University of Denver; and Kathy Kelly, Co-founder, Voices for Creative Non-violence. The percentage of civilian deaths to combatant deaths varies according to the article, and there is no consistency on this. The panel estimated 50 civilians' deaths for every desired target, but other articles don't place the estimates this high. See also Craig Whitlock, "Drone Strikes Killing More Civilians than US Admits, Human Rights Groups Say," *The Washington Post*, October 21, 2013; William Saletan, "In Defense of Drones," from an anti-drone protest at the Nomination of John Brennan as CIA Director; "By the Numbers: World-wide Deaths," from the National WWII Museum in New Orleans, LA, n.d.; "A Profile of the Modern Military," Pew Research Centers, Social and Demographic Trends Project, 2011; "Fact Box: Military

and Civilian Deaths in Iraq," *Business and Financial News*, December 15, 2011.

27. Barry Schweid, "Bush Was Unready for Postwar Iraq, Panel Concludes," Associated Press, July 27, 2005. Also see Congressman Martin T. Meehan, press release, "Meehan: New Report Shows Mismanagement of Iraq War Is Weakening Military," July 22, 2004; Robert Parry, "Iraq War's Two Constants," consortiumnews.com, August 13, 2005; Kelley Beaucar Vlahos, "Bush Supporters Question Iraq War Tactics," Foxnews.com, September 12, 2005; Griff Witte, "Halliburton's Higher Bill: Rising Costs Reflect Growing Demand for Firm's Services," *Washington Post*, July 6, 2005; John Connly Walsh, "Big Disappointments in Iraq," *The Spectator*, August 10, 2005; and "Estimates Costs of Iraq War: War in Iraq Could Cost up to $9 Billion Monthly, says CBO"—August 8, 2005. From Congressional Budget Office.

28. Dr. Rachel M. MacNair, "History Shows: Winning with Nonviolent Action," Xlibris Corporation, 2004, pp. 10, 17.

29. Christian Aid, *Pocket Prayers for Peace and Justice* (London: Church House Publishing, 2004).

Chapter Seven
Confronting Terrorism and Fear

1. Matthew 24:7.
2. Luke 21:11.
3. I Peter 3:6.
4. I John 4:18.

5. Psalm 23.
6. Psalm 91.
7. Psalm 91.
8. Isaiah 51:12.
9. Ezekiel 11.
10. Psalm 128, Proverbs 14, Job 28.
11. Psalms 34, 55.
12. I John 4:18.
13. Matthew MacWilliams, "The Best Predictor of Trump Support Isn't Income, Education, or Age. It's Authoritarianism," *vox.com*, February 23, 2016.
14. From the "Beyond War" seminars held in the 1980s and 1990s. I attended several of these seminars in Los Angeles, California, in the 1980s.
15. Psalm 23.
16. God came to earth as a little child. Other verses relating to this include Matthew 18:1–6, Luke 18:17.
17. Luke 10:29–37.
18. Luke 15:8–10.
19. Matthew 23:37, Luke 13:34.
20. Matthew 5:46–47.
21. Matthew 5:43–44; Luke 6:27, 6:35; Romans 12:20.
22. Koran 5.8, "The Dinner Table."
23. I Samuel 17.
24. John 9.
25. Matthew 12.
26. Durland, *God or Nations*, p. 163.
27. Ibid.
28. John 8.
29. Hosea 8:7, Galatians 6:7.
30. Matthew 6:26. Much of this is discussed in Durland, *God or Nations*, p. 165.

31. Durland, *God or Nations*, p. 166.
32. This theory is discussed in more detail in my book *Web-Thinking: Connecting Not Competing for Success* (Maui, Hawaii: Inner Ocean, 2002).
33. Kat Kane, "Hillary Clinton Just Outlined a Plan to Defeat ISIS and Global Terror. 3 Things you Need to Know," and Elizabeth Chan, "Hillary Clinton Just Showed Why Defeating ISIS and Welcoming Syrian Refugees Aren't Opposing Ideas," *hillaryclinton.com*, November 19, 2015.
34. From the commentator of the family videos of the Kennedy family.
35. Quoted in Jim Wallis, *God's Politics: Why the Right Gets It Wrong and the Left Doesn't Get It* (San Francisco, Harper San Francisco, 2005), p. 88.

Chapter Eight
Secrets, Lies, and Deceptions

1. Matthew 5:33–37.
2. Matthew 23:23.
3. Huckabee made this statement at a visit to Winthrop University in 2015 and also following the Michigan Primary, January 15, 2008.

Chapter Nine
Crossing the Political Divide

1. Some of these verses include Romans 12, I Corinthians 12, I Corinthians 13.

2. William A. Galston, "Democrats and Republicans Agree on More Than You Think & Why That Matters for 2016," *brookings.edu*, January 22, 2015.

3. Raymond Hernandez and Patrick D. Healy, "Oddly Hillary and, Yes, Newt Agree to Agree," *New York Times*, May 13, 2005; also "A Good Idea from the Odd Couple," from the Editorial Desk, *New York Times*, May 16, 2005.

Index

COLOPHON

Typefaces used in the second, third, and fourth editions of
Jesus Rode a Donkey are Constantia and Optima; the title page
contains Bernard MT Condensed and League Gothic.

Text is set in Constantia, a serif font with old style numbers
designed by John Hudson for continuous text in either print or
on-screen uses, released in 2004 and featured in the Microsoft
ClearType Font Collection.

Display type is Optima, designed by Hermann Zapf in the 1950s
for the D. Stempel AG Foundry in Frankfurt, Germany. It can
be found in many contexts—corporate and political campaign
logos, as well as the engraved names of missing and dead at
the Vietnam Veterans Memorial and the National September 11
Memorial & Museum.

On the title page, the book title and author are set in Bernard
MT Condensed, a Microsoft font based on designs from the
Bauer foundry, similar to Bernhard Antiqua Schmalfette (bold
condensed), and to designs from the Monotype Corporation.

The subtitle and edition line are set in League Gothic. Designed
by Morris Fuller Benton for the American Type Founders
Company in 1903, League Gothic is now in the public domain.
The version used in this book has been revised and updated
with contributions from Micah Rich, Tyler Finck, and Dannci,
who contributed extra glyphs.

12.16

CPSIA information can be obtained at www.ICGtesting.com
Printed in the USA
BVOW06s0255290616

453859BV00003B/10/P